estherpress

Books for Courageous Women

ESTHER PRESS VISION

Publishing diverse voices that encourage and equip women to walk courageously in the light of God's truth for such a time as this.

BIBLICAL STATEMENT OF PURPOSE

"For if you keep silent at this time, relief and deliverance will rise for the Jews from another place, but you and your father's house will perish. And who knows whether you have not come to the kingdom for such a time as this?"

Esther 4:14 (ESV)

What people are saying about …

Through the Desert

"Lina is one of the clearest communicators I know when it comes to the tangible hope and steadfast peace available to Christ followers because of God's faithfulness, regardless of what's going on within or around us. And I can't think of a more necessary and relevant message for modern culture in light of the difficulties, disruptions, and acrimonious division we've experienced over the past few years. This study provides a deep dive into a refreshing, biblically sound oasis for anyone who finds themselves feeling weary or parched!"

Lisa Harper, doctorate in progress, Bible teacher, conference speaker, and author of *Life*

"By unpacking helpful biblical narratives, *Through the Desert* provides powerful perspective for anyone navigating a desert place. You're bound to see the undeniable faithfulness of God again and again, and come away changed."

Ruth Chou Simons, *Wall Street Journal* bestselling author, artist, and founder of gracelaced.com

"Boom! Lina is in her God-given sweet spot with this study. One of the greatest life lessons is learning not to waste your pain. Lina teaches everything you need to know about your desert experiences with clarity, passion, and practical application. The best part of this study is Lina's unflinching conviction that faith in God alone will get you through—it's true."

Karl Clauson, pastor at 180 Chicago Church and host of *Karl and Crew Mornings* podcast

"Instead of fearing, dreading, or avoiding the inevitable desert seasons of life, *Through the Desert: A Study on God's Faithfulness* will leave you anticipating intimacy with God, growth in God, and gifts from God that can only come from the desert. Lina takes us on a journey that reveals the relentless goodness, mercy, and love of God toward us. God is forever faithful, even in the desert places."

Christine Caine, founder of A21 and Propel Women

"Author and speaker Lina AbuJamra gently guides us through the many deserts of testing, brokenness, and waiting we encounter. She grounds us in theological truths and points us to the One who will lead us through the wilderness, to a path of healing, and to eternal life through Christ Jesus. For those of us who feel like we are walking through a dry season, this Bible study is like water to our souls, inviting us to experience God's faithfulness and unconditional love as we track with the arc of God's promises fulfilled in Scripture."

Joyce Dalrymple, JD, pastor, lawyer, and host of *Adopting Hope* podcast

"There are few people I would trust to lead me through my desert places, but Lina is one of them. Her honesty about the struggles we all face in our Christian walk are matched only by the hope she offers us from the Scripture. If you're in a wilderness place right now, pick up this study, take Lina's hand, and let her guide you to Christ."

Hannah Anderson, author of *Turning of Days*

"As a pastor and ministry leader I have had hundreds of conversations where people confide that they are 'going through desert.' They typically see the desert as a negative place to be in. In her study *Through the Desert*, Dr. Lina with clarity, insight, and practical applications points us to the transformative power of these desert times and God's unfailing faithfulness in the dry places. If you or a friend are in 'the desert,' I strongly encourage you to dive into this study and discover not only how to survive the desert but God's purpose and plan to use your desert experience for good."

Dr. Mark Jobe, president of Moody Bible Institute

"This study is accessible and encouraging. It encouraged me where I think we all most struggle: simply with faith and trust in God. In the end, do I believe the God of the Bible is good? Do I trust His promises? Can I walk with Him through darkness, believing there is light around the corner? Lina takes us through stories of Scripture we are all most likely familiar with, but she does it in a way that reminds us, not of what we need to do, but of who our God is and what we can count on from Him. If you need encouragement to persevere in faith, Lina is a trustworthy friend on that journey."

Wendy Alsup, author of *I Forgive You* and *Companions in Suffering*

Through the Desert

A STUDY ON GOD'S FAITHFULNESS

AN INTERACTIVE
BIBLE STUDY
Includes Six-Session
Video Series

LINA
ABUJAMRA

Through the Desert

A STUDY ON GOD'S FAITHFULNESS

📍 MAPPING THE FOOTSTEPS OF GOD SERIES

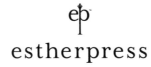

estherpress

Books for Courageous Women
from David C Cook

THROUGH THE DESERT
Published by Esther Press
an imprint of David C Cook
4050 Lee Vance Drive
Colorado Springs, CO 80918 U.S.A.

Integrity Music Limited, a Division of David C Cook
Brighton, East Sussex BN1 2RE, England

Esther Press, David C Cook, and related logos are trademarks of David C Cook.

ISBN 978-0-8307-8421-9
eISBN 978-0-8307-8422-6

© 2023 Lina AbuJamra

The Team: Susan McPherson, Jeff Gerke, James Hershberger, Jack Campbell, Michael Fedison, Susan Murdock
Cover Design: Emily Weigel
Interior Map: Dale Meyers
Author Cover Bio Photo: Jake Preedin

Printed in the United States of America
First Edition 2023

1 2 3 4 5 6 7 8 9 10

102022

To my mother, who first taught me about Jesus
then showed me what it looks like to love Him most dearly.

Contents

Meet the Author

Lina AbuJamra is a pediatric ER doctor, now practicing telemedicine, and founder of Living with Power Ministries. Her vision is to bring hope to the world by connecting biblical answers to everyday life. A popular Bible teacher, podcaster, and conference speaker, she is the author of several books, including *Thrive*, *Stripped*, *Resolved*, and her most recent book, *Fractured Faith*.

Lina is ministering to singles through her *Today's Single Christian* show on Moody Radio and is engaged in providing medical care and humanitarian help to refugees in Lebanon, Ukraine, and others in disaster areas. Learn more about her at livingwithpower.org.

Acknowledgments

I am deeply grateful for my agent, Don, who saw more potential in me than I felt at the time the idea for this book came to be.

The message of this book was birthed over the course of a lifetime. I have had several companions along the way who have reminded me of the gift of the desert: Diana and Irina continue to hold me to the truth. My mother is the steadiest example of "faithful obedience in the same direction" that I know. Sam is always near to remind me that every little word matters and that Jesus is always faithful.

I'm grateful to every woman who has listened to me teach. Your support and encouragement have shaped my calling. Thank you to the Living with Power Facebook community for your continuous support.

For the team at David C Cook—thank you for believing in me and giving me a chance to dance for Jesus. Teaching the Bible is the heartbeat of my soul. Thanks to Susan McPherson, Jeff Gerke, and the entire marketing team for creating something out of my words.

Lastly, and always, I thank the Lord Jesus Christ, the lover of my soul, for carrying me through the desert. You have always been and always will be faithful to me.

Introduction

Do you have any idea how many women's Bible studies are published each year? A lot! Which means that no one really needs another Bible study. What we need is a fresh move of God. What we need is a deeper encounter with Jesus. What we need is to be awakened to spiritual realities and to understand what's really going on in our lives. The good news is that this is exactly what we've been created for. God wants an intimate relationship with us, His people. He gave us His Holy Word because He wants us to hear His Word and to know His heart.

If this is your first Bible study, welcome. I'm really glad you're here. You probably don't have too many expectations yet. You're in the perfect place to allow God's Spirit to shape you through His Word.

But if you're like me and you've been in a million Bible studies before, let's make a commitment together right now. Even though you don't know me very well yet, by the time this study is over, we'll be best friends. So let's resolve to approach this Bible study with the expectation of encountering God in a deeper way than we'd hoped or imagined. Let's expect God to change us through this study.

No one really needs another Bible study. What we need is a fresh move of God.

In many ways, I'm no different from you. I'm short on time and high on expectations. I want to be taught deep things of God without having to dedicate my entire life to doing so.

I want a teacher who is funny enough to keep me entertained but deep enough to keep me from feeling like I'm in just another fluffy women's Bible study. I want the study to be high on content and low on nonsense. Too much theology, and I'll think it's irrelevant. Too little theology, and I'll wonder if the teacher is legit.

Do you want to know what's really awesome? I won't be able to ruin this Bible study for you even if I tried. It's the Holy Spirit of God who is our teacher when it comes to God and His Word. I'm merely the instrument in the hands of the Redeemer, to use Paul Tripp's phrase. What you will get out of this study will be in direct proportion to the space you allow the Spirit of God to speak into your life.

There are four things you need to know about me as we begin our journey together:

1. If you see me on video, you'll notice that I speak fast—but I enunciate every word really well. Don't let my pace mess with you. You're up for the task. I promise.

2. I can be pretty intense—but I'm never mad at you. I was born in Lebanon to Lebanese parents, and it shows. My people speak fast and furiously about everything from religion to the weather. Nevertheless, we're good people.

3. I am an ER doctor—but I'm never in a rush. ER docs get a bad rap for being too direct and too rushed. While I do tend to think in bullet points, I'll never find a problem I won't try to solve. I'm also really good at simplifying difficult problems. You will thank me for this later.

4. I am single—and I'm okay with it. Don't try to set me up with your single uncle—unless he is really good looking, has zero baggage, and knows how to cook.

For better or worse, God has allowed our paths to intersect for the next six weeks. I'm so glad He did, and I'm thrilled you're here. I am praying for you and can't wait to see all that God is going to do in your life as we dig deeper into His Word together.

Lina

About This Study

This study is about God's faithfulness to us in our desert places.

From the very first pages in Genesis, we see that God created a place called earth, and then He created humans to inhabit the earth. Starting with the garden of Eden and all the way to the book of Revelation, we observe the importance of *place* in the relationship between God and His people. Land matters to God. Location matters to God. Throughout the Bible, God allows His people to wander through wilderness places, eventually making it to the Promised Land.

The Bible tells the story of God's people in all sorts of places. Sometimes they're stuck in prisons, and other times they're surrounded in battle. Sometimes God's people are seen soaring on mountaintops, and other times they're caught trudging through the valleys. Yet no matter where God's people find themselves, one thing is evident: God remains faithful to His people. God remains true to His promises no matter how hard the road becomes. Eventually, God's people learn that His faithfulness matters more than the places they find themselves in.

Our backdrop for this study will be desert places. After the introductory lesson, we will spend five weeks following the footsteps of God and His people in five different desert places:

- Week 1: Introduction to the study.
- Week 2: Abraham is invited out into the desert in obedience to God's promise.
- Week 3: The people of Israel are sent into the desert after leaving Egypt.
- Week 4: The people of Israel find mercy in the desert in a season of deep darkness.

- Week 5: John the Baptist shows us the gift of the desert by living out his calling.
- Week 6: Jesus teaches us how to live as overcomers in our desert places.

Our goal will be to focus on God's faithfulness to His people in desert places. Though we will get to know a number of amazing people of the Bible each week, the hero in our study will not be one of the many characters of Scripture. The hero in this study is God. He is the one we will focus on. He's the one we will seek to understand. He's the one who will give our lives meaning and dimension.

How It Will Look

Through the Desert is a six-week Bible study. It is my hope that you'll be doing this study with a group in person or online because you'll get the most benefit from sharing your answers with others in the discussion time. But if you're doing this as an individual study, the same structure to the sessions will apply.

Each session begins with a brief overview of what we'll be studying for the week. Then, during your group's meeting time, you'll watch a video of me teaching the basis for the lesson. Fill in the blanks by watching the video and discuss it together using the video group discussion questions. If you're on your own, answer the questions in your workbook.

You can structure your group's meeting time however you'd like, but here's a sample flow to the meetings to get you started:

- Snacks and fellowship as you gather
- Greeting and introduction
- Opening prayer
- Recap discussion of the previous week's homework (except for session 1)
- Watch the video (fill in the blanks as you watch)
- Video group discussion (either discuss as a group or complete on your own)
- Prayer requests (for individual study, you may want to start a prayer journal)
- Closing prayer and dismissal

When you go home, you'll begin your daily interactive material on your own. Each week has five days of material in which we dig deeply into God's faithfulness to His people in the desert places. At the end of each week, you'll find a section called "Praying through Scripture," where you'll place yourself in the sandals of the people of the Bible and really soak in the passages we're studying.

At the end of this book, I've placed some helpful resources:

- a leader's guide with tips for guiding a group through this study
- the answers to the fill-in-the-blank questions from the videos
- a QR code as a quick link to all the videos
- the endnotes

Note: The final session won't have any homework. You'll gather to watch the video, discuss it, and maybe you'll want to celebrate together!

If you've ever found yourself in a desert place, this study is for you. Perhaps you're stuck in a spiritual desert right now. My prayer is that God will reveal Himself more clearly to you through this study and that you will begin to sense His presence even more deeply as you dig deeper into the reality of who He is through His Word.

Let's do this!

Session 1

Introduction

Genesis 1–2

Watch the session 1 video now. The video is available at DavidCCook.org/access, with access code DesertPlaces.

1. The story of the Bible is the story of God and His _____ to His people.

2. The story of God's faithfulness is best understood by mapping His footsteps and presence with His people in _____ _____.

3. The story of God is never without _____ and is always deeply personal.

Video Group Discussion Questions

After watching the video, discuss the following questions in your group.

📍 In Genesis 3:9, God finds Adam and Eve and asks them this question: "Where are you?" How would you answer Him if He were to ask you that question today?

📍 Think about where God has placed you right now. What kind of place is it? Do you long to leave it or can you see God's faithfulness in it?

📍 How can you understand God's faithfulness to Adam and Eve even though He threw them out of the garden of Eden?

📍 In the video, Lina said, "The story of God is not a story with me as its hero." How did you react to this statement? How have you made studying the Bible about you in the past?

📍 The story of God is deeply personal. In what ways have you experienced God personally? Where in your life do you long to experience Him even more?

Faithful

faith·ful | \ ˈfāth-fəl \

Definition of *faithful*

> **1:** steadfast in affection or allegiance: LOYAL // a *faithful* friend
>
> **2:** firm in adherence to promises or in observance of duty: CONSCIENTIOUS // a *faithful* employee
>
> **3:** given with strong assurance: BINDING // a *faithful* promise
>
> **4:** true to the facts, to a standard, or to an original // a *faithful* copy
>
> **5:** *obsolete*: full of faith[1]

Faithfulness has to do with being reliable. It has to do with fidelity, firmness, stability, trustworthiness, trueness to one's word, and dependability. While no earthly person is 100 percent faithful, the Bible teaches that God is 100 percent faithful in all He does in accordance with His divine character. The fact that God is faithful is one of the most reassuring attributes about Him.

We are going to build on our understanding of the faithfulness of God in the weeks to come. For now, take some time to pray, asking God to show you where in your life you say you believe God but where your heart is far from trusting Him yet.

Typically, our struggle is in our desert places, but the good news is that God is committed to getting us through those desert places stronger in faith. He's a God who is that good.

He's a God who is faithful!

Week 1: Invited into the Desert

Deuteronomy 7:9
"Know therefore that the LORD *your God is God, the faithful God who keeps covenant and steadfast love with those who love him and keep his commandments, to a thousand generations."*

Introduction

"Trust me," he said. I was in Colorado and had just signed up to go on one of those adventure zip line things across a huge canyon. The canyon was wider than anything I'd ever set my eyes on. I looked at my guide, then looked at the vast opening in front of me and wondered for the umpteenth time what had possessed me to follow him so blindly. I heard the clip of the harness being tightened around my waist but still couldn't wrap my mind around the notion that in just a few minutes I would be putting my life into the hands of a man I barely knew and a thin piece of rope hanging from the edge of the mountain.

"Trust me." Two of the most overused yet undervalued words in the English language. You've heard the used-car salesman promise you that you're not buying a lemon—"Trust me," he says. You've looked into the eyes of your doctor who promises it's not going to hurt that much—"Trust me," she tells you. You've had parents and spouses promise you they would never leave you or harm you, but an unexpected death or a tragic divorce has left you reeling.

Trust me.

I grew up in west Beirut, Lebanon, during one of the worst civil wars my birth country has gone through. I was taught from a very young age not to trust anyone. That pattern has followed me throughout much of my life. When I hear the words "trust me," I roll my eyes.

"Prove it," I whisper under my breath. "Show me you're worthy of my trust first, and then I'll think about it."

Maybe you're like me. You struggle with trusting others. You've been there and done that. You've given away your trust too quickly and have been deeply burned because of it. You've learned to keep your guard up. You've learned to watch where you're going, to double-check the harness two or three times first, or maybe you've decided to skip the ride altogether.

Here are some of the most common reasons we struggle with trust:

- You've trusted people who have disappointed you completely.
- You've been taught from a young age that no one can be trusted.
- You've been hurt before and don't want it to happen again.
- You had expectations that were unmet by others.

Sadly, our trust issues with other humans have a tendency to erode our relationship with God. When God tells us to trust Him, it's no surprise that we struggle with it. We've been trained to doubt. We've been trained to keep our guard up. We've been taught that sooner or later people will let us down.

Though we're talking about trusting God now, deep down most of us aren't sure God will do all He has promised. His Word seems too good to be true in a world that is broken. The truth is, we're afraid to trust God. What if God lets us down? What if the miracle we're hoping for doesn't take place? At the first sign of difficulty, we want to cut and bail.

"I shouldn't have trusted so easily," we tell ourselves. "Why did I ever think things would be different?"

Deep down, even though we say we believe God, most of us really struggle with trusting Him. In this study, I hope to help you understand what's behind our trust issues with God. Peace in the Christian's life flows out of a heart that trusts God even when everything in life points against Him.

In this week's homework, we're going to spend time with the first guy who truly learned to trust God: Abraham. In Genesis 12, God called Abraham to follow Him, and Abraham did. What's amazing about the story is that right after God made Abraham an incredible promise, Abraham was invited to leave the comfort of home and head into the desert. I suppose you can say that God's invitation to Abraham was to learn to trust Him in the desert places. Abraham's life did not turn out to be easy, but it was rich—so rich that we're still talking about him today.

Our goal this week is to begin to understand the connection between God's promises to us and our ability to thrive in desert places. Our ability to make it in desert places rests on our willingness to hang on to God's promises. The more familiar we become with God's promises to us, the easier it will be for us to trust Him in the desert. But it all starts with God's promise to us.

> Our ability to make it in desert places rests on our willingness to hang on to God's promises.

Remember that the hero of our story is not Abraham. It's God! It's God's footsteps we're tracking throughout the pages of Scripture. It's God's faithfulness we're focused on. When our Christianity hasn't lived up to our expectations, it's important to stop and figure out why. The more we understand who God is, the more we become convinced of His goodness even in our most difficult circumstances, and the easier it will be for us to say yes, as Abraham did, when He asks:

"Will you trust Me?"

Day 1: Father Abraham

Reading: Genesis 11:27–12:9

Theme: God invites me into the desert to get to know Him better.

My favorite movie growing up was *The Sound of Music*. I watched it eighteen times before I graduated from high school. Who am I kidding? It's still my favorite movie. Are you impressed? You should be! At one point in the movie, Maria the governess sings a song that says: "Let's start at the very beginning, a very good place to start."

I agree with her. If we're going to grow in trusting God, we have to start at the very beginning. While our introductory lesson focused on Adam and Eve, this week we're going to spend our time in Genesis 12. We're going to become familiar with the story of Abraham, our forefather, and learn how God taught Abraham to trust Him.

But here's the first thing you need to know: It all started with a promise. It was a promise that propelled Abraham from the comfort of home into the wild of the desert. It was this promise that would change the course of Abraham's life. It was this promise that awakened Abraham to the reality of God and His presence in his life. It's a promise that continues to impact your life and mine today.

In order to better understand what I mean, read Genesis 11:27–12:9. Summarize in your own words what God's Word says.

One of the most important tools in studying the Bible is to learn where the text falls in the biblical narrative. In other words, let's get some context.

Read Genesis 11:27–32 and jot down a sketch of Abraham's family tree.

Check out this map of Bible lands in Abraham's day.

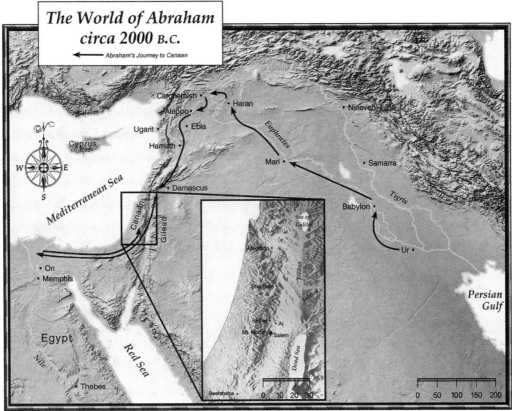

Locate the place where Abraham came from, Ur of the Chaldeans, and trace his journey all the way from the land of Haran to the land of Canaan, where God had called him to go.

Abraham's life wasn't perfect. Even before God called Abraham out of Haran, he had some struggles.

📍 Identify some of the problems in Abraham's life before God called him to leave home.

The world Abraham was living in was also challenging. Let's get a feel for the cultural context that Abraham was living in during those days. Look up these Bible passages for help:

- Genesis 11:1–9
- Joshua 24:2

While the whole world was worshipping idols and false gods, God Almighty made Himself known to Abraham with a promise. In Genesis 12:1–3, God reveals the promise. This promise is called a covenant. It's impossible to understand the biblical narrative without understanding the covenant God made to Abraham in Genesis 12:1–3. So much of what we believe about God is rooted in this covenant. But before we break down the Abrahamic covenant a bit more, read the text again and pick out what it was about Abraham that caused God to choose him out of all the humans on the planet to become the father of His chosen people.

Did you find anything?

Check again.

Still nothing? You're right.

The story of God choosing Abraham tells us a whole lot more about God and His goodness than it does Abraham's worth. This is a key principle in growing our trust in God:

God chooses us not because we are good but because He is good.

📍 Let's make this a little more personal. Can you summarize your life in a few lines? What are some of the highlights and tragedies that characterize your family of origin? Is there anything about your life that caused God to call you to Himself? If so, what?

Now let's dig deeper into the covenant God made to Abraham, referred to today as the Abrahamic covenant. This covenant was first made in Genesis 12:1–4, then reiterated in Genesis 15. It's the first of eight covenants God makes to His people.

In Old Testament days, a covenant had a few essential elements to it. It was made between two or more parties. It was a binding commitment that involved an oath. It typically had some symbol or physical sign associated with it, and it involved a witness. God's promise to Abraham was unique in that it was an unconditional covenant that hinged only on God's faithfulness. Abraham didn't have to earn it. He simply had to receive it.

> *God chooses us not because we are*
> *good but because He is good.*

There were three elements to the promise God made Abraham. See if you can pick them out in Genesis 12:3.

What are the three things God promised Abraham?

- The Land
- The Blessing
- The Child

Scholars have defined *covenant*—translated from the Hebrew *berith* and the Greek *diatheke*—in various ways, and the context in which the word is used in Scripture will also inform our understanding of its meaning. At its most basic level, a covenant is an oath-bound relationship between two or more parties. In divine covenants, God sovereignly establishes the relationship with His creatures. A divine covenant given after the fall is fundamentally one in which God binds Himself by His own oath to keep His promises.[2]

Genesis 15 gives a critical illustration of the unconditional nature of this promise. Read Genesis 15:12–21. What was Abraham's part in the making of this covenant?

Doesn't it give you a deep sense of relief to know that when it comes to God's covenants to us, He expects so very little of us? He simply expects us to trust Him!

Before we end our time together today, let's go back to Genesis 12:1–3 and focus on God's promise to Abraham. At the heart of the promise was the answer to Abraham and Sarah's one major problem in life: they could not have a baby. Enter God and His promise that Abraham and Sarah would indeed have a child. Yet despite God's promise to Abraham, no son would be born to this old couple until more than twenty-five years later.

Can you see the disconnect between Abraham and Sarah's reality and what God had promised them? What emotions do you feel as you contemplate this disconnect?

It turns out that your trust in God will usually grow the most in the areas where you feel the most pain.

Let's Make This Personal

What is the most painful place in your life right now? As you think about God's promises *to you*, is there an area in your life where it feels like God's promises don't match up with the events in your life?

Today's Take Home Point

God's goodness is meant to be
received in the midst of your pain, not
proven by the absence of pain.

Final Thought

As you consider God's promises to you and your own barren places, what might God be inviting you to in your present painful situation?

Day 2: Leap of Faith

Reading: Genesis 12:1–9

Theme: Following God by faith means stepping out into the unknown.

I was engaged—twice. The first time, I ended the engagement two weeks before the wedding. The second time, I had learned some lessons and was smart enough not to wait as long to call things off. I mention this to say that when someone invites you on a journey for life, it usually takes two to make it happen. First comes the invitation, then comes the response to the invitation.

In both my engagements, I had thought I knew the guys I was thinking about marrying. I knew a lot of facts about them. I knew enough about their character to say yes. Have you ever wondered about cultures that believe in arranged marriages? While it might make the dating process easier, how does one actually commit their life to someone they have never met? I'm sure you have a list of answers and wisdom about marriage for me, but I assure you I'm asking the question rhetorically.

In Genesis 12, that's exactly what happened, though. When God chose Abraham and called him into covenant with Him, Abraham barely knew God. In light of what Abraham knew about God, his response to God is nothing short of amazing.

Let's read Genesis 12:1–9 again. Ask the Holy Spirit to show you something new in the text today. Don't skip the reading simply because you read it yesterday. Take time to soak in God's Word. See what new things God might be pointing out to you through this passage today.

Focus on verse 4, where Abraham's response is neatly summarized. Write down the first half of the verse below:

"So Abram went, as the LORD had told him."

I have the gift of complicating things in my life. For Abraham (formerly known as Abram), it wasn't that complicated. God said it, and Abraham did it. If you don't fully appreciate the leap of faith that Abraham took on that day, check out what the writer of Hebrews says about it.

⚲ Read Hebrews 11:8. Write down the second part of the verse. According to God's Word, did Abraham have any idea where God was leading him? What do you think gave him the courage to step out in faith anyway?

⚲ Has there ever been a time in your life when you stepped out by faith in obedience to God not knowing where you were going? How did that feel?

It's important to understand why Abraham did what he did. It's easy to assume that he obeyed God in order to receive God's favor, but that's not what God's Word tells us happened. The covenant God made with Abraham was unconditional, meaning that it all depended on God. Abraham's obedience was not a necessary step for him to get the reward of a son. Abraham's obedience was born out of an encounter with God that stirred something so deep and powerful in him that the thought of taking a leap of faith wasn't as scary as you and I imagine it would be.

The apostle Paul summarizes Abraham's story in Romans 4. It's an incredible passage of Scripture that you might want to spend extra time in today.

⚲ Read Romans 4:13–25. Underline how many times the words *faith* and *believe* show up in the text. How much did Abraham know about God's faithfulness when he obediently stepped out in faith?

⦿ What do you think was the tipping point that caused him to take a leap of faith and believe God?

Leaving Haran was not an easy step for Abraham. In fact, it was quite costly for him to move. Review Genesis 12:5 and think about what it cost Abraham to say yes to God. Furthermore, Abraham didn't leave Haran alone—he brought his whole tribe with him. Have you ever considered how your decision to follow the Lord has impacted the people around you?

⦿ What are some of the reasons people hesitate in saying yes to God? List some of the common excuses people have for not following God's call.

Faith is such a big part of the Christian life that you could even say faith *is* the Christian life. What I've observed in my life is that I often believe in God but lack trust in Him. Intellectually, I agree with all that God says in His Word. Yet there is a canyon a mile wide between my head and my heart. My trust in God must move past my intellect to my emotions and my will. Trusting God is meant to lead me to action and to change.

⦿ In what area in your life do you struggle to trust God?

God understands that though most of us start our faith journey with unshakable faith, we soon question God and wonder about His promises. It's because God understands our struggle that He gives us His promises to hang on to. God's promises are intended to accompany us on our journey through the desert. God is so committed to growing our trust in Him that, over and over again, He does everything possible to grow our trust in Him.

Even more amazing is the truth that God is faithful to us even when we struggle to believe Him.

Faith is such a big part of the Christian life that you can even say that faith *is* the Christian life.

Read Psalm 100:5—"For the LORD is good; his steadfast love endures forever, and his faithfulness to all generations."

What does the psalmist mean when he says that God is faithful? How often is your definition of God's faithfulness based on your understanding of your own faithfulness?

God's faithfulness does not mean our lives will be problem-less. In fact, God makes no apology for how difficult the road will be.

Read Genesis 15:13. What does God promise Abraham will happen to his descendants down the road?

Perhaps fear is one of the biggest reasons many hesitate in saying yes to God. Life with God was never meant to be easy, but the promise we hang on to in our desert places is that God is faithful to us even when life is hard.

Let's be honest: If I were Abraham and Sarah, I would have expected God to fulfill His promise for a son right away. I would have expected to receive the promise of the land not long after giving up my home in Haran. I would have expected at least some immediate gratification. Instead, God invited Abraham into the unknown desert.

It turns out that God's idea of building our trust in Him is different from ours.

Let's Make This Personal

📍 What was it about God's invitation *to you* that prompted you to say yes to Jesus? What did you know about God when you said yes to Him? How did your decision affect your family and tribe?

📍 Have you ever believed God enough to change? What are the most radical ways your life has changed since accepting the invitation to follow Jesus?

📍 Have you ever felt disappointed in God for allowing you to suffer even though He has informed you of the difficulties ahead in desert places? As you deepen your understanding of God's faithfulness, how can you confess to God how you might have misjudged Him and reached wrong conclusions about His goodness to you?

Today's Take Home Point

God longs for far more for us than we do. He knows that as much as we want to see the fulfillment of His promises to us, the biggest gift He can give us is the gift of Himself.

Final Thought

⚲ Where in your life right now is God inviting you to make radical changes?

Day 3: Old and New Covenants

Reading: Hebrews 8:6–13 and Jeremiah 31:31–34

Theme: While God's faithfulness to Abraham is seen through the Old Covenant, His faithfulness to us is best seen through Jesus Christ.

I was in my second year of medical school when I got a flip phone that I could use while driving. My dad, who thought he was ahead of his peers, had a phone in his car—as in the phone was actually attached to the console of the car. It was a thing back then. I remember feeling so proud of my new flip phone. I walked around for days thrilled with the new technology sitting in my pocket.

Before you assume I'm one hundred years old, just ask your mom about it. She knows what I'm talking about. Anyway, you can imagine my awe when in 2007 the first iPhone came out. Steve Jobs became an overnight hero, and today we can't imagine a world without portable smartphones.

While my old fancy flip phone and my current amazing iPhone are both phones, one is far better than the other. Today, living without my smartphone isn't an option. It's changed my life completely.

When it comes to God and His promises, there are some things that will never change. God is the same yesterday, today, and forever. He is still faithful. His Word is still true. He still never makes mistakes. He cannot lie. He does not make a promise that He will not keep. His character does not change.

But some things do change with time. Some things are eventually replaced with something better. I'm talking about God's covenant here. Think of that first covenant like the original version of the iPhone. Throughout the Old Testament, we learn about several newer versions of God's covenant to His people. There was the Mosaic covenant at Sinai (Deut. 11) and the Davidic covenant (2 Sam. 7:8–16). But best of all was the covenant given to us in Jeremiah 31, which affects you and me today: the New Covenant!

So, even though God doesn't change and His promises don't change, some things do become better with time.

When it comes to God's covenant to His people, the best news in the world is that even though Abraham was given that first covenant, which changed his life, God has something even better for us. We miss God's blessing if we limit our understanding of God's faithfulness to the story of Abraham. Though God's promise to Abraham was nothing short of amazing, we need more than the promise of an Isaac to hang our faith hat on. If we're going to make it through the desert today, we need a New Covenant. We need Jesus.

We're going to spend some time getting a little more familiar with the New Covenant. But first, let's make the connection between God's promise to Abraham and His promises to us today.

♀ Read Galatians 3:13–15. Who is the link between the Old and the New Covenants?

♀ Read Hebrews 8:6–13. According to God's Word, which covenant is better, the Old or the New? Why?

♀ What did God do to the Old Covenant once the New came about?

Do you know anyone who still has a flip phone? Even my father, before he died, got rid of his first-generation phone and bought himself a beautiful iPhone. He didn't need his old car phone anymore. There was a new and improved phone for him to use. The same applies to God's promises to us. God's faithfulness continued well past the story of Abraham. While

God fulfilled all His promises to Abraham, He also used Abraham and Abraham's descendants as the means through which God's Son, Jesus, would someday be born into this world. It is through Jesus that God's goodness extends to us too.

Today, you and I can hang on to Jesus in our desert places. He is the one we've been promised who will get us through the badlands.

Hebrews 8:6–13 refers to one of the most important passages in the Old Testament. We will spend more time studying Jeremiah 31 in week 3 of this study, but let's get acquainted with it right now.

📍 Read Jeremiah 31:31–34. Underline and count how many times God uses the phrase *I will* in these verses. Who can you conclude is responsible in making and keeping this New Covenant?

📍 What are some of the blessings of the New Covenant based on Jeremiah 31:31–34?

So many of us are disappointed in God because we believe He hasn't given us the things that we want and think we need. I've made that mistake before. I've assumed that God's faithfulness to me is proven by His willingness to give me the things I deeply desire—for a while, it was a husband and kids, then it was a successful ministry, and now I long for a secure and comfortable life.

As long as we build our belief in God's goodness on what we want instead of what He has actually promised, we will inevitably be disappointed. God's faithfulness is not defined by

God doing what I want Him to do. Rather, God's faithfulness is His trustworthiness based on His ability and willingness to keep His covenant to us. The key is to understand His promises to us and to live in light of them. God's faithfulness is His ability to help us get through our desert places by giving us *Himself.*

The promise God made to Abraham was so much bigger than simply the birth of his son Isaac. It was the promise of the coming of the Messiah, Jesus Christ, through the seed of Abraham. The good news for us today is not simply that God kept His promise to Abraham and gave him a son in his old age, but that God through Abraham gave us Jesus, the mediator of an even better covenant!

Extra Credit

Let's take a moment and compare the Old and the New Covenants. The more familiar we become with God's promises for us, the stronger our trust in God's goodness and faithfulness will be![3]

Old Covenant	New Covenant
Earthly (Heb. 9:1)	Heavenly (Heb. 8:1)
Copy and shadow pointing to the work of Christ (Heb. 8:5; 9:23; 10:1)	Real (Heb. 9:24) and true (Heb. 8:2; 10:1)
Featured human priests who were destined to die	Possesses a high priest who lives forever (Heb. 7:28)
Priest had to offer sacrifices for his own sins (Heb. 9:7)	Jesus' sinlessness meant that He did not offer sacrifice for Himself (Heb. 9:14)
Multiple priests had to enter the sanctuary repeatedly to offer numerous sacrifices (Heb. 9:6-7; 10:11)	A single high priest, Jesus, entered the heavenly sanctuary once (through His death and resurrection) and offered a singular sacrifice once and for all time (Heb. 9:12, 26; 10:10, 12)

Contained the sacrificial blood of animals (Heb. 9:18–22)	Jesus offered His own blood (Heb. 9:12, 26)
The worshipper could not be perfected (Heb. 9:9)	A process of moral transformation enacted that completely purifies (Heb. 9:14; 10:14)
The people were brought to God only symbolically	People can *actually* approach God with boldness and without fear (Heb. 4:16; 10:19)
Written on tablets of stone (2 Cor. 3:3)	Written by the Spirit on tablets of human hearts (2 Cor. 3:3; Heb. 8:10)
Brings condemnation since the law cannot be kept (2 Cor. 3:9)	Brings righteousness and life through Christ, who fulfilled the law's requirements (2 Cor. 3:9; Rom. 7:24–25; Rom. 8:1)
Fading, temporary glory (2 Cor. 3:11)	Lasting, permanent glory (2 Cor. 3:11)
In spite of all God's works, His people did not know His ways (Heb. 3:8–10)	All God's people will know God personally (Heb. 8:11)
"I will be their God, and they shall be my people" is at the heart of the Old Covenant (Heb. 8:10)	"I will be their God, and they shall be my people" is at the heart of the New Covenant as well (Heb. 8:10)

Take a look at all you've been promised in Christ. It's pretty incredible, right? The more grounded we stay in God's promises to us, the deeper our joy will be. The more familiar we become with God's promises to us, the greater our confidence in Him will be.

Remember that the Bible is the story of God and His faithfulness to His people despite their unfaithfulness to Him. The more we review that story, the stronger our hope will be.

♦ Though it's only our third day going through homework, we've already learned so much. Take a moment to write down your favorite verse from today's lesson.

Speaking of smartphones, you might even make that verse your wallpaper for the day. In an age of unprecedented distractions, we need to fix our minds on the truth of God's Word and the reality of His abiding presence with us in order to make it through our desert places.

Let's Make This Personal

📍 How has your idea of God's faithfulness been impacted by your unanswered prayers and past disappointments?

📍 How does understanding that Jesus is our hope remove any sense of disappointment in unfulfilled dreams?

Today's Take Home Point

The biggest mistake we make in Christianity is to make ourselves the center of our story. Jesus is the answer to all of our hopes and dreams. When we have Him, we have everything.

Final Thought

📍 As you consider the Old Covenant versus the New Covenant, what new idea or promise is God inviting you to embrace?

Day 4: Sacred Places

Reading: Genesis 12

Theme: The more you're willing to step out in faith based on God's promises, the more of God's faithfulness you will experience.

There are some locations in life that stand out like no other.

The first place where I encountered God deeply was in northern Wisconsin, smack-dab in the middle of nowhere. I was sixteen and had moved from Beirut, Lebanon, to Green Bay, Wisconsin, a year earlier. I went to a Christian camp for two weeks. That's when my life changed.

I don't remember what the pastor spoke about that night, but I remember having a keen awareness of God's nearness and presence. I stood outside the chapel under the glittering Wisconsin night and sensed God calling me to Himself. Though I'd accepted Jesus a few years earlier, that night at camp changed my life. It was the first time I truly experienced God and started to understand His love for me more personally. I committed my life to Him that night. I resolved that He would become the first and most important thing in my life.

That location became a sacred place for me. It felt as if, in that moment of divine awareness, an altar was raised in my heart. I freely offered my life as a living sacrifice to God that day. The desire to experience God intimately has remained my deepest longing.

If you had told me on that night how challenging life with Jesus would be, I might not have believed you. I couldn't have predicted the seasons of pain and disillusionment that would follow. I never would have imagined that the desert would become such a normal part of my Christian life. The only thing I knew for certain on that night was that God loved me unconditionally and had called me to Himself.

I had decided to follow Jesus—no turning back, no turning back.

Have you ever had a deep spiritual encounter with God? Take a moment and describe your sacred place here.

Today's lesson will focus on the importance of sacred places in our relationship with God. For you, perhaps that sacred place is the quiet of the early morning while your kids are still sleeping. Or maybe your sacred space is your commute to work. Or perhaps your sacred space has yet to be created. God has a way of meeting us where we least expect Him to. He speaks in ways we cannot predict or imagine. Those places where we encounter God deeply become sacred spaces in our hearts.

Read Genesis 12 again. Let's dig deeper and ask the Lord to reveal some things today that we may have glossed over in the last days of homework.

○ How old was Abraham when he left his home in Haran?

○ Where did God tell Abraham to go?

○ Who did Abraham take with him?

○ What was the main problem facing Abraham and Sarah in those days?

Go back and check that biblical map showing Abraham's trek from Haran to Shechem. Do you know much about that journey? Let's find out about it together.

Distance between Haran and Canaan: 400 miles

Topography: desert

Distance between Shechem and Bethel: 20 miles

Distance between Bethel and Egypt: 225 miles

⦿ What do you think might have gone through Abraham's mind as he made his way across 400 miles of desert trying to track God's promises? What emotions do you think might have filled his heart?

⦿ Have you ever been asked by God to follow Him somewhere without clear directions? What emotions filled you during those days?

Something miraculous had happened to Abraham. Something significant had propelled him to move from the comfort of home to a strange land. Something massive enough had occurred to convince Abraham and his family to leave everything they knew and follow this God they had just met.

⦿ What do you think might have been the reason Abraham was willing to move from the comfort of home to the unknown future?

Take a look at these verses and note repetitive words and concepts:

> Genesis 12:1—"Now the LORD said to Abram"
> Genesis 12:4—"as the LORD had told him"
> Genesis 12:7—"Then the LORD appeared to Abram and said"

Can you identify the miracle that had taken place in Abraham's life in Genesis 12?

When was the last time you heard God speak to you clearly and unequivocally? How close to miraculous do you believe this is?

Sometimes I get caught up in theological debates about God's voice. Most Christians recognize that God speaks to His people through His Word, the Bible. But there are differing opinions on whether God speaks to us audibly. No matter where you stand on this debate, the most awe-inspiring and amazing reality I have ever encountered is that God speaks to us at all. Imagine how life would look like without any communication from the Almighty. Imagine what kind of relationship we would have with God if He didn't speak to us.

We serve a God who speaks! On the first pages of Genesis, God speaks the world into existence. After breathing man into being, God speaks to him and gives instructions for life and marriage. After Adam and Eve's fall, God finds them and speaks to them with a piercing question. The first thing God does when He calls Abraham to Himself is to speak to him.

◉ If you're feeling frustrated because you've never heard God audibly speak to you, take heart. You need to better understand how God speaks. For each of these verses, write down how God communicates with us today.

Hebrews 1:1–3

Romans 10:17

2 Timothy 3:16–17

Hebrews 4:12

John 10:27–28

The miraculous, awesome reality is that we serve a God who speaks to His people through His Holy Scriptures. It was God's words to Abraham that turned Abraham's life upside down. It was God's Word that turned my life upside down too. However, there are seasons in my life when it becomes harder for me to hear God's voice.

◉ Do you ever struggle to hear God's voice too?

◉ What are some of the most common reasons it might be hard for you to hear God's voice?

♥ Read Genesis 12:7. This is the second time that God spoke to Abraham in Genesis 12. What did God tell Abraham in Genesis 12:7?

It seems as if the more Abraham pursued God, the more he heard from God. It was after Abraham stepped out in faith that God revealed more of His promise to Abraham. Initially, God had told Abraham simply to go. Now, God tells Abraham exactly where the Promised Land is. Sometimes we wait for God to tell us the details of His plans for us when all He's asking is for us to trust Him with what He's told us so far. *As we learn to step out by faith on God's promises, He reveals more of His plans to us.*

We're finally getting to sacred places! The miracle of God speaking was not lost on Abraham. Abraham was so moved by the intimacy of his relationship with God and the reality of God's voice in his life that he built an altar to God right there at the oak of Moreh, where God had clearly spoken to him. This was not the only altar Abraham would build to God. In fact, altar building became something Abraham did regularly. Abraham learned to celebrate God by building altars for Him. Each altar Abraham built was a chance to celebrate the faithfulness of God to him.

I love Oswald Chambers's commentary on Genesis 12:8 from *My Utmost for His Highest*:

> Bethel is the symbol of communion with God; Ai is the symbol of the world. Abraham pitched his tent between the two. The measure of the worth of our public activity for God is the private profound communion we have with Him. Rush is wrong every time; there is always plenty of time to worship God. Quiet days with God may be a snare. We have to pitch our tents where we shall always have quiet times with God, however noisy our times with the world may be. There are not three stages in spiritual life—worship, waiting and work. Some of us go in jumps like spiritual frogs, we jump from worship to waiting, and from waiting to work. God's idea is that the three should go

together. They were always together in the life of Our Lord. He was unhasting and unresting. It is a discipline, we cannot get into it all at once.[4]

For Abraham, building altars became symbolic of his deepening experience with God. While the Old Testament building of an altar became symbolic for commemorating an encounter with God and a place for offering sacrifices for sins, in the New Testament, God gave us an even better way to worship through Jesus Christ. In the New Testament, we no longer have to build altars to commemorate our encounters with God, because Jesus makes our heart His home.

♥ Read 1 Corinthians 6:19. What do you learn about sacred places here? In what sacred place does God's Spirit abide since the advent of Jesus?

♥ Read Romans 12:1. Based on this verse, how does the New Testament believer offer an altar of worship unto God?

Let's Make This Personal

♥ What are some of the sacred places where you have encountered God?

9 What are some ways you can make yourself a living sacrifice to God?

9 As you think about all God has done and said to you in this season in your life, what are some of the things you can celebrate on the altar of worship to God?

Today's Take Home Point

A life of consecration to God begins in our
hearts as we wake up to God's presence,
His faithfulness, and His promises.

Final Thought

9 Oswald Chambers powerfully wrote that worship is giving God the best that He has given you. What might God be inviting you to give to Him today?

Day 5: Famine in the Land

Reading: Genesis 12:10–20

Theme: It is God's faithfulness in the famine that rescues us from more pain.

I'm a Peloton fanatic. I won't bore you with the details, but I am attracted to the tougher bike rides on the Peloton app. I like interval training and high-intensity training. It's supposed to make me stronger, and I can tell by how I feel today compared to a few years before I got on that bike that I am indeed stronger.

Here's one thing I've learned after hundreds of Peloton rides: I've never started a ride that I didn't question midway through. It's true. I choose rides that I know will make me stronger and that I am convinced are good for me, but halfway through, as I huff and puff and sweat my body weight off, I question why I got on that bike to begin with.

What makes Peloton a great exercise program is that the teachers are fully aware of my problem. They know my tendency to want to quit. They understand exactly what it will take to make me into the kind of athlete they know I can be. So, midway through the bike ride, I hear the same reminders echo through the speaker:

"If you're wondering why you got on the bike today, you're doing it right!"

"If you're asking yourself why you're doing this, it's because you want to get stronger."

"Don't quit. It's supposed to be this hard. If you think this is tough, you are tougher."

I'm not trying to sell you an exercise program here, but I am trying to make a point. Now that we've laid the foundation for our study, today we start digging into the desert places. Most of us intuitively understand that difficult seasons are for our eventual good. Deep down, we know that it's the hard road that makes us stronger. Easy is for toddlers. If you want to grow in your walk with Christ and into full maturity, the road needs to get harder. And in order for your faith to stand strong, you're going to have to learn to walk through desert places without quitting.

While I intellectually understand these principles, I've found that I often prefer to be coddled. I want a God who will help me feel good and who will keep the road easy and flat. I resist the hills and somehow imagine that my life ought to be the exception to the rule of life.

Perhaps Abraham fell for that same wishful thinking. If he did, he wouldn't be the first or the last person to struggle with his faith in the midst of an unexpected desert. In today's reading, we're going to study how Abraham reacted to a famine in the land. While Abraham opted for an easy way out, it was God's faithfulness to Abraham that saved the day.

⚲ Read Genesis 12:10–20. How did Abraham respond to the famine that hit the land?

⚲ What surprises you about Abraham's response?

⚲ Does his reaction to the famine seem consistent with his response to God's call earlier in Genesis 12?

Up until this point, we've witnessed Abraham responding to God's voice in his life. When God called, Abraham followed. Where God pointed, Abraham went. This time, though, when famine hits, Abraham moved with no clear directive from God. He made the 225-mile journey from Bethel to Egypt hoping to find food in his desert place. He made the 225-mile journey to Egypt because he was afraid.

⚲ What do you think went through Abraham's head as he made his way toward Egypt?

Egypt is the biblical symbol of worldliness and bondage for the people of Israel. In week 2 of our study, we will study the people of Israel being freed from the bondage of Egypt, a place that becomes associated with sin and death. Yet it is in Egypt where Abraham begins to more fully understand God's faithfulness to him.

Let's dig deeper into the story.

📍 Summarize the events that transpired in Genesis 12:10–20.

📍 What was Abraham's harebrained plan to find food in the famine?

📍 What would you have done if you were in Abraham's shoes?

📍 What was God's response to Abraham's lapse in judgment?

📍 Does God's response surprise you? Why or why not?

📍 Our decisions always impact the people around us. How do you think the Egypt episode affected Lot the nephew of Abraham? (See Genesis 13 and 19 for more about Lot.)

It's amazing when you think about it. Abraham initially stepped out with a giant leap of faith in God, yet just a few verses into his story, he is paralyzed with fear. The same man who had erected two altars of consecration to God now finds himself running to Egypt for help.

Have you ever wondered why God didn't stop Abraham? Have you ever wondered why Abraham didn't ask God for more direction? The truth is that we've all been there before. The longer I live as a follower of Jesus, the more grateful I am for the story of Abraham's reaction to the famine in the land.

I'm beginning to see that the story of Abraham's faithlessness tells us more about God's goodness than it does Abraham's weakness. It is God's desire to reveal His faithfulness to us, and there is no better place for God to reveal His faithfulness than in the places of our fear. There is no better place for us to stand secure in God's faithfulness than when we've been rescued by God in the places of our failure.

In other words, *the best place for God to reveal His love for us is in the place we least deserve it.*

After my mountaintop experience with God in northern Wisconsin, things went smoothly for a season. But it didn't take long for famine to come. I wish I could tell you that I had learned from Abraham and turned to God in my desert places. But like Abraham before me, I turned to Egypt in my fear. I looked for ways to satisfy my own hunger in the areas of my need. Like

Abraham before me, I let go of all the promises that God had so generously provided for me to rest in. I overestimated my need to provide for myself and underestimated the depth of God's faithfulness to me.

At the end of the day, I suppose I didn't really understand God's faithfulness yet. Some days, I still don't. But there is one thing I've learned for sure: we will never experience the faithfulness of God as we will in our seasons of famine. It's in the desert places of our lives where God's promises sustain us the most. It turns out that the desert places are just as sacred to God as the places where we have built our altars of worship to Him.

Let's Make This Personal

What kind of famine have you faced in your life?

Where have you looked for help in famine? How many of your reactions were rooted in fear?

How does God's faithfulness to Abraham affect your response to Him in your areas of failure and famine?

Today's Take Home Point

The best place for God to reveal His love
for us is in the place we least deserve it.

Final Thought

📍 What is God's invitation to you today as you consider your present places of famine?

Praying through Scripture—Week 1
Into the Unknown
Genesis 12:4–9

> So Abram went, as the LORD had told him, and Lot went with him. Abram was seventy-five years old when he departed from Haran. And Abram took Sarai his wife, and Lot his brother's son, and all their possessions that they had gathered, and the people that they had acquired in Haran, and they set out to go to the land of Canaan. When they came to the land of Canaan, Abram passed through the land to the place at Shechem, to the oak of Moreh. At that time the Canaanites were in the land. Then the LORD appeared to Abram and said, "To your offspring I will give this land." So he built there an altar to the LORD, who had appeared to him. From there he moved to the hill country on the east of Bethel and pitched his tent, with Bethel on the west and Ai on the east. And there he built an altar to the LORD and called upon the name of the LORD. And Abram journeyed on, still going toward the Negeb.

Read the passage out loud once.

Now close your eyes and take a few deep breaths. Pray with me: "O God, I pray that You will help me to hear You speak during this time of meditation on Your Word. I open my hands to You. I open my ears to You."

Pause for eight to ten seconds.

Imagine yourself in Abraham's shoes. You've been told by God to move, but you're not sure where to go. You call for a family meeting and inform your loved ones that you intend to follow God. They ask you where you're going. You answer honestly that you're not sure. You invite them to come with you.

How do you think they respond? What do you tell them to convince them to go with you?

What was it about your encounter with God that turned everything upside down? Why can't you just go about living your life as usual? What questions do you have for God?

Read the passage again.

Pause for five to eight seconds.

Imagine with me that you've packed everything up and you've started the journey. It's hot, and you're thirsty. You're not 100 percent sure which direction to go. You say a silent prayer and take the next step. Your knees hurt a bit, but you're on the go now. There's no turning back.

What are your fears? What are your frustrations? Where is God in your imagination now? What do you hang on to as the sun sets on that first day of travel? What questions are you having to answer from the people on the journey with you? What are your last thoughts as you drift into sleep?

Pause five to eight seconds.

One day, you find a big oak along the way. You camp out for the night. That night, God appears to you again. What goes through your mind? How does His presence affect you? How do you feel about your life the next morning? Why do you build an altar to God that next morning?

God's manifest presence reminds us that we are not alone. No matter how deep our questions in life are, all it takes for us to find hope again is a fresh word from God. What if we understood from this story that God's voice is loudest in our life when we need it the most? What if we associated our deepest, darkest nights with the ideal place for God to speak?

Now close your eyes and take a few deep breaths. In what area in your life do you have questions about your future? Where in your life do you long for clear direction from God? If you're unsure of what next step to take, spend some time jotting down what God has promised you so far. Ask God to give you the courage to take the next step and the direction you're to go.

Session 2

Invited into the Desert

Genesis 12:1-9

Watch the session 2 video now. The video is available at DavidCCook.org/access, with access code DesertPlaces.

The desert is a place where I must rely on God's promises and trust His faithfulness. A place of dependence. It is a place I never intended to be in and that I long to get out of.

1. It is impossible to understand God's faithfulness without understanding His _____.
2. It is impossible to experience God's faithfulness without _____ His covenant.
3. It is impossible to make it to the Promised Land without walking through _____ _____.

Video Group Discussion Questions

After watching the video, discuss the following questions in your group.

📍 How does understanding God's covenant to His people affect your understanding of God?

📍 Has there ever been a time in your life when you stepped out in faith in response to God's invitation to you?

📍 In what ways has your life changed since you took that first step of faith to follow God?

📍 What could you learn from Abraham's detour in Egypt that would help you live differently?

📍 How might God's favor on Abraham in Egypt radically transform your view of God's faithfulness to you?

Week 2: Purpose in the Desert

Hebrews 10:23
"Let us hold fast the confession of our hope without wavering, for he who promised is faithful."

Introduction

This might come as a surprise to you, but in my younger years I used to be a Girl Scout, and yes, I survived it! My favorite part was our overnight camping trips. Even though I lived in war-torn Beirut in those days, we had a handful of rare and wonderful weekends where it was safe enough to go camping with our Girl Scouts tribe. We would drive up to the mountains and pitch our tents for the weekend. I even had my own metal canteen for the event. We went all out.

When evening came, our leaders would assign us our overnight duties. I remember waking up as a twelve-year-old sometime after midnight to take my turn in the night watch. It was the scariest thing I'd ever done. I had no idea who might attack our camp or what animal might chew me up in the middle of the night.

Now let's be real. In hindsight, it wasn't like the safety of the entire tribe depended on me. I was too young and too weak to do anything about any attack that might come upon us. I would later find out that I was never alone on these night watches. Our leaders were awake too. They were still in charge. They knew every detail of every movement at that campsite. And even though they knew that my night shift wasn't the dealbreaker for our safety, they also knew that my courage would dramatically increase as a result of my time in the darkness of the night.

They understood that strength is born out of adversity and confidence grows under pressure.

We've been tracing the footsteps of God through the desert in an effort to grow in our understanding of His faithfulness to us. We spent last week focused on God's promise to Abraham as the catalyst for Abraham's move from his place of comfort into the desert. We started to flirt with the idea that God's plan for us to thrive in the desert is closely associated with our ability and willingness to hang on to His promises to us.

Strength is born out of adversity and confidence grows under pressure.

In this week's teaching, we're going to continue following the footsteps of God through another desert place. We will deepen our understanding of God's faithfulness to His people. This week, we will shift our focus from Abraham to Abraham's descendants, the people of Israel. We'll be spending most of our time in the book of Exodus this week, starting in Exodus 13:17–22.

Day 1: Why the Desert

Reading: Exodus 13:17–22

Theme: God has a purpose in the desert places of our lives.

Have you ever tried to locate a place on Google Maps? If you punch in the address and see the pin drop, you'll get a pretty good idea of where that place is, but you'll have no idea where it is relative to where you are. In order to better understand the location, you will need to zoom out a bit, and then maybe even a bit more.

Trying to understand our reading for today would be like trying to understand that pin drop without context. We need to get our bearings as we move from the story of Abraham in last week's homework to the story of his descendants in the book of Exodus.

But first, let's go back to Genesis for a moment.

📍 Read Genesis 15:13–14. What did God prophesy to Abraham about his offspring?

📍 What span of time would Abraham's offspring spend in the foreign land?

📍 Now jump to Exodus 1:1–5 and Exodus 12:40–42. Based on these verses, how true to His word was God?

You may or may not be very familiar with the story of the Patriarchs. To bring you up to speed, let me try to summarize four hundred years of history in a few bullet points:

- Abraham and Sarah had a son named Isaac, exactly as God had promised.
- Isaac married Rebekah and had twins named Esau and Jacob.
- The twins were a bit of a mess.
- Jacob was the chosen one selected to carry the legacy of Abraham. He had twelve kids, who would become the leaders of the tribes of Israel.
- Jacob's life was long and painful with detours and desert places along the way.
- Jacob's favorite son was Joseph, whom God eventually used to move Abraham's family to Egypt—through an excruciatingly painful ordeal.
- Joseph was sold as a slave by his brothers to strangers and ended up in Egypt, while his brothers lied to Jacob, telling him that Joseph was killed by an animal.
- Joseph spent a long time in slavery, until God fulfilled his dream.
- Joseph became the second in command to Pharaoh and eventually provided a place of refuge for his now-repentant brothers.
- The entire family of Jacob—all twelve great-grandkids of Abraham—ended up spending 430 years in Egypt, exactly as God had predicted they would.
- Those years in Egypt served to form a nation, just as God had promised Abraham.

I think I did really well, don't you? Now let's zoom in to the events in the book of Exodus.

Read Exodus 1:8–14. Summarize the situation for the people of Israel. Where was God during this desert season?

◉ Now read Exodus 2:23–25. What do you learn about God's faithfulness here?

As much as I adore Moses, for the sake of our study, I'm going to skip over his story. God, after all, is the hero of our story. Tracking His footsteps in desert places throughout the scope of Scripture is our goal, so forgive me the unpardonable feat of moving quickly past the story of Moses. Instead, let's fast-forward a little until we get to Exodus 12. We're picking up the story after the ten plagues, landing on the final plague—the death of the firstborns—and the story of the Passover.

◉ Read Exodus 12:1–13. In the final verse of this section, what was the reason God passed over the people of Israel and their children and spared their lives?

◉ Read Hebrews 9:11–12. In the New Testament, what replaces the blood of the Passover lamb?

◉ In what way is the sacrifice of Jesus better than the sacrifice of the lamb?

📍 Read Exodus 12:29–32. Comment on God's faithfulness to His people in the story so far.

Now let's zoom in even more to our text for this week, Exodus 13:17–18. We've been building to this point, so lean in a little as you ask the Lord to open your eyes to fresh insights.

📍 Read Exodus 13:17–18. List the reasons God chose to lead the people of Israel to the desert instead of using the alternate shortcut.

Sometimes the most obvious truths are the ones we forget. What we learn in theory evaporates as we live our lives practically. Though the people of Israel have seen a whole lot of God's power so far, and though they are well versed in the history of their forefather Abraham, they are going to flounder for years to come in the practical practice of daily living.

What starts out as a simple journey from Egypt to Mount Sinai is going to turn into the prolonged story of the people of Israel in a repetitive cycle that will become more familiar to us as we study God's faithfulness to His fickle people.

What's amazing about what we're going to learn is that none of the disasters that are to come and none of the temptations in the desert and none of the failures of the people of Israel will come as a surprise to God. He already knew exactly how the whole story would play out.

We have now set up the framework for our time together this week. We've covered a lot of important ground that will help us dig deeper into God's purpose for us in the wilderness.

Let's Make This Personal

⚲ Think about the desert you are going through right now. Write down one or two areas in your life where you're walking through a desert place.

⚲ How would it change your perspective if you knew that God had intentionally placed you in that wilderness?

Today's Take Home Point

The desert is not an oversight in God's plan for my life but an integral part of my growth process.

Final Thought

God is too faithful to withhold from us the riches of the desert places in our lives.

Midbar and *Arabah*—Biblical Wilderness

Words translated as "wilderness" occur nearly three hundred times in the Bible. A formative Hebrew memory is the years of "wandering in the wilderness," mixing experiences of wild landscape, of searching for a promised land, and of encounters with God.

The wandering described in the Pentateuch (the first five books of the Bible) takes place in the *midbar*: uninhabited land where humans are nomads. This common Hebrew word often refers to a wild field where domesticated animals may be grazed and wild animals live. This is in contrast to cultivated land. Hence, *midbar* is sometimes translated "the pastures of the wilderness" (Joel 1:19–20). Another word for wilderness is *arabah*, translated in some versions as "desert" (Gen. 36:24). Here's a verse that uses both words: "The land that was desolate [*midbar*] and impassable shall be glad, and the wilderness [*arabah*] shall rejoice" (Isa. 35:1 DRA).

Two other Hebrew words for wilderness include *chorbah*, land that lies waste, and *yeshimon*, land without water.[5]

Day 2: Compass Points

Reading: Exodus 13:20–22 and Exodus 14:19–20
Theme: We have everything we need to make it through the desert.

I know I could make it through this difficult season if God would just give me more direction! Have you ever caught yourself thinking something like that?

Most of us recognize that the Christian life is hard. We assume that it would be easier if God would send us more specific details on what to do next.

You might be familiar with the tale called *Pilgrim's Progress*, the classic book by John Bunyan. The protagonist is Christian, a young man who, as his name suggests, becomes a Christian.

The story is an allegory of the Christian walk. It traces Christian's path from the City of Destruction (i.e., the world), to the Celestial City (i.e., heaven). On his way to the Celestial City, Christian meets all sorts of characters who shape his life. He meets folks like Obstinate and Pliable, and others like Worldly Wiseman and Goodwill. He also walks through a variety of terrains, like the Slough of Despond and the Village of Morality.

On and on the story traces the path of Christian as he walks through wilderness after wilderness, until he finally makes it to the Promised Land. And slowly, throughout the pages of this small book, we observe Christian transform into a man of strength and maturity, influenced by good friends like Hopeful and Faithful.

While most believers comprehend the facts of the Christian life, we are like Christian in *Pilgrim's Progress* in that most of us struggle with its reality. We want direction. We want answers. We want comfort and ease and to be free from suffering. We want God to show Himself more clearly to us when we do find ourselves in the middle of the desert.

Yet it is the desert that awakens us to our need of God and sets us in a place of utter dependence on Him. Simply put, the desert serves a purpose. God's aim is to use the desert places in our lives to make us stronger. But how? That's where we will focus our attention today.

📍 Let's pick up where we left off yesterday. Read Exodus 13:20–22. Who accompanied the people of Israel when they left Egypt?

📍 Read Exodus 14:19–20. What role did the cloud and fire play for the people of Israel in the desert?

Note that both the pillar of cloud by day and the pillar of fire by night did not appear to the people of Israel until they'd left the bondage of Egypt—and that the pillars eventually stopped appearing once the Israelites made it to the Promised Land. There is great symbolism here for the New Testament believer.

📍 What is significant about the timing of the appearance of the pillar of fire and the pillar of cloud in the history of the people of Israel?

The pillar of cloud/fire is considered a *theophany*. A theophany is a manifestation of God in the Old Testament.[6] God's presence guided the people of Israel and protected them from the enemy.

Don't you wish we had a pillar of cloud by day to lead us and a pillar of fire by night to protect us today? Don't you wish we had a theophany guiding us around?

The desert awakens us to our need of God and puts us in a place of utter dependence on Him.

You might be relieved to know that we've been given something even better than a pillar of cloud by day and a pillar of fire by night! We've been given so much more.

Old Testament stories stand as a shadow of things to come. They offer an illustration of what we as New Testament believers can experience even more deeply. Just as the New Covenant replaced the Old Covenant in a far superior fashion, so God's presence in cloud and fire was replaced by something—or someone—far better. While Old Testament believers needed a cloud by day and a fire by night to experience the presence of God, we have been given Jesus, who is the manifestation of God the Father, and the Holy Spirit, who abides in us as our guide and our light in the darkness.

Our problem is a problem of awareness. So let's become aware of the compass headings God has given us today to guide us through our desert places. For each verse, write down how God still guides us today:

📍 Read John 16:7. What does Jesus promise about His provision for us after His departure?

📍 Read John 16:13. What is one of the roles of the Holy Spirit?

📍 Read Acts 2:3–4. What does fire symbolize at Pentecost?

◉ Read 1 Corinthians 12:12–13. What do these verses teach about the timing of the Holy Spirit's coming?

◉ Read Psalm 119:105. What other means of lighting our path have we been given?

◉ Read John 14:8–9. Why did Philip fail to connect God's presence with Jesus? What do you think Philip was expecting?

Let's Make This Personal

◉ Describe an area in your life right now where you feel you have no guidance or direction from God.

◉ How aware are you of the path God has given you to travel through the desert?

◉ What stands in the way of seeing God's presence in your life?

◉ How yielded are you to the Holy Spirit?

◉ What areas of your life must you change to allow God's Spirit to lead you more powerfully?

Despite the fact that the people of Israel had the pillar of cloud by day and the pillar of fire by night, their track record for trusting God in the wilderness was not great. We, too, fail to trust His goodness despite God's manifest presence in our lives. We are prone to wander and prone to fear. Yet despite the people of Israel's inability to see God's goodness and heed His compass headings, God still led them through the desert day after day after day.

The longer I walk the path of faith, the more I am reminded that Christianity has less to do with how much I believe God and more to do with His faithfulness to me. Though the pillar of cloud by day and the pillar of fire by night were awesome miracles declaring God's faithfulness and abiding presence to His people, the greater wonder is the miracle of God's faithfulness to His people even when they didn't deserve it. God is just as committed to proving His faithfulness to you as He was to the people of Israel in their journey out of Egypt.

Today's Take Home Point

God will never lead you where His
grace will not sustain you.

Final Thought

📍 What compass heading is God inviting you to become more aware of today?

Day 3: Facing Our Fears

Reading: Exodus 14:1–20

Theme: God gets great glory when we trust Him in our deepest fears.

When was the last time you got on a plane for a flight? I bet you didn't even think twice about it. But stop for a second and consider the facts: every time you get on a plane, you willingly put yourself in a box of metal that will hang in the stratosphere defying gravity, and you trust the skills of a pilot, whom you've never met and will never even see, to get you from point A to point B.

It's a miracle. It truly is.

As long as the flight is smooth, most of us ignore the details of what's happening in the air or the miracle that allowed us to participate in this crazy phenomenon. But if you've ever hit turbulence on a flight, you've probably questioned your sanity for putting yourself in that metal box to begin with. The confidence you had strutting down the tarmac is long gone the minute the pilot's voice is heard on the overhead speakers reminding you that he is, indeed, just a man in a metal box trying to get you from point A to point B without crashing. The stronger the turbulence is, the louder your fear becomes. And the more likely revival is to break out in the skies. Have you ever noticed how many people cry out to God in the middle of turbulence?

Trials are much like turbulence. One minute, you're excited to be storming out of Egypt, Pharaoh in your rearview mirror, but in the moment when you hit the turbulent Red Sea, everything changes. That same pillar of cloud that's supposed to be leading you by day becomes a dense fog obstructing your vision. That pillar of fire you were hoping would lead you by night becomes a reminder of all you left behind in the comfort of your Egyptian shack.

I've been there. It's amazing how quickly the afterglow of my last encounter with God evaporates in the face of my next big desert moment.

We are a people whose knee-jerk response in life is to fear, despite all the proof we've been given that our God is faithful. We so quickly forget that the same God who has brought us through our last wilderness has led us to this present wilderness for a reason. His design is for us to get stronger. His plan is to teach us to trust Him even more with every new desert experience.

It's time we learned to deal with the Red Sea moments of our lives, and today is a good day to start doing it.

Our text for today is Exodus 14. Take a couple of minutes to read it.

God has just delivered the people of Israel from Egypt, so they have every reason to be confident in God. But they're about to face the Red Sea. Though they have all the facts they need to stay strong, their hearts—like ours—are prone to fear.

♀ Summarize Exodus 14 in a couple of sentences.

♀ Whose idea was it to bring the people of Israel to the edge of the Red Sea (v. 1)?

♀ What reason does the text give for the trial that was facing the people of Israel (v. 4)?

♀ Have you ever thought about the glory of God? Christians love to talk about the glory of God, but what exactly does it mean?

◉ How would you define God's glory in your own words?

The word *glory* comes from the Latin word *gloria* and means "fame" and "renown."[7] It is used in the Bible to describe the manifestation of God's presence as perceived by humans. Glory is the invisible qualities of God made visible. I like to think of the glory of God as our "Wow, God" moments.

◉ How was the Red Sea experience an opportunity for God to get glory over Pharaoh through the people of Israel?

In Exodus 14:4 we're told that it was God who hardened the heart of Pharaoh. We like to think of God as our benevolent Father, never allowing harm to come our way. The first time I was faced with the notion that God might lead me toward the wilderness on purpose, I was mad and confused. I am still sometimes baffled by God's ways. The idea that God would lead me beyond the edge of my comfort with the enemy at my back seems cruel. Yet the more I experience God's goodness in the desert, the more I begin to understand that, as Joni Eareckson Tada says, "God allows what he hates in order to accomplish what he loves."[8]

In my mid-twenties, I ended my first engagement two weeks before the wedding. Shortly after that drama, the other guy I thought I would marry told me he had moved on and found someone else to spend the rest of his life with. It felt like a Red Sea moment. Even though there was no enemy behind me, it felt hard to admit that God had somehow allowed me to arrive at this place of deep pain. It was difficult to understand how God could have spared me my pain but did not. One day, I was reading the Minor Prophets when I came across this passage in Hosea.

📍 Read Hosea 2:14–15. Write down how these verses inform your knowledge of God when you're in a desert place.

The most precious gift God gives us in our darkest deserts is the gift of intimacy with Him. His tenderness flows out of our surrender to the idea that His leading us to the wilderness is not an act of His anger toward us but quite possibly His most loving act toward us. That same God who delivered us from Egypt and led us to the edge of the Red Sea is more than faithful to rid us of our fears and deliver us from our enemies, if we would but learn to trust His heart toward us.

📍 Read Exodus 14:10–12. What emotions characterize the people of Israel in this moment?

📍 What do their words reveal about their hearts?

The desert is the place where our words often betray our hearts. What we believe about God becomes evident through the words that flow out of our mouths when we're in the wilderness. God uses our desert places to reveal the state of our hearts to us.

How did Moses react to the fear in his people? Write down his words from Exodus 14:13.

What do you think gave Moses his courage?

Moses stood his ground in faith. Perhaps because he had been in his own wilderness for forty years before he had learned some things about God's faithfulness. Or perhaps he understood what most of us forget: that it would be inconceivable that the same God who had led the people of Israel this far would abandon them in this moment.

The most precious gift God gives us in our darkest deserts is the gift of intimacy with Him.

Think about it. God had heard the groanings of the people and delivered them from Egypt. He had shown His power through ten massive plagues. He had provided a pillar of cloud and of fire to guide His children. What were the odds that this same God would simply lead His people to the edge of the Red Sea and then allow them to die?

You're right. The odds were slim to none that God would do that! Are you starting to believe that the God who led you this far is not about to abandon you? He has purpose in your desert place. He offers you peace in your fears.

What happened next is one of the greatest miracles in the entire Old Testament. The people of Israel numbered almost a million. Exodus 12:37 tells us that there were six hundred thousand men leaving Egypt, not counting women and kids. God was not hindered by the masses of people. He simply parted the Red Sea and escorted them through it one by one by one. Not one of them was forgotten. Not one of them died.

♥ Read Exodus 14:30–31. Something radical happened to the people of Israel. They had started out fearing their enemy. Who did the people of Israel fear now that they had crossed the Red Sea?

Sadly, the people of Israel's elation in God's goodness didn't last very long. In the next few days, we will learn more of their story. It seems hard to believe that a miracle as massive as the parting of the Red Sea wouldn't have had a lasting impact on God's people. After all, how many Red Sea experiences will it take for us to trust God without wavering? More than one, it seems! Perhaps one of the reasons God continues to send us into the wilderness is because He understands just how fickle our hearts truly are. One of the reasons God continues to invite us into the desert is because He longs to show us over and over again just how deeply He loves us.

What is it that makes you afraid? Where do you long for a parting of the Red Sea in your life? Maybe it's time you see that fear's greatest gift is that it brings us to our knees. Won't you stand still and see this salvation that the Lord is working for you today?

Let's Make This Personal

♀ What are you most afraid of?

♀ Are you facing a Red Sea moment in your life right now?

♀ What do the words coming out of your mouth in your present trial reveal about your trust in God?

♀ List some of the miracles God has done in your life to get you to the place you're in. Are you willing to believe that the same God who got you this far will get you through your desert place?

Today's Take Home Point

The same God who got you this far will
get you through your desert place.

Final Thought

⚲ What is God's invitation to you today in the places where you are most afraid?

Day 4: Desert Songs

Reading: Exodus 14:15–31 and Exodus 15:1–21

Theme: Even in the desert there is room for rejoicing.

We're in a study about God and His faithfulness to His people when they find themselves in desert places. In this week's homework, we've been trying to better understand why God allows His children to go through the desert. God wants us to trust Him more. The more unshaken we remain in our desert places, the greater His glory. The more we believe His promises when life looks grim, the higher we exalt Him.

As a Bible teacher, I have spent a big portion of my time teaching women about why God allows suffering in our lives. I've taught a lot of lessons exhorting women to persevere in the waiting. Lately, I've noticed that I've spent so much time adjusting to delays and detours and deserts that I've left little time to rejoice in God's answers to my cries for help. Perhaps some of my reticence in rejoicing has been my self-made strategy to protect my heart from more pain. I'm afraid to get my hopes up. I'm afraid to believe that God might in fact give me the breakthrough I long for.

When breakthrough does come, we need to be sure we spend time celebrating.

Today's lesson is one of rejoicing. It's a lesson about dancing and singing our hearts out to the Lord in our desert places.

While the people of Israel weren't out of the wilderness yet, today's lesson will allow us to see that even in our desert places, God has miracles in store for us. Breakthroughs do come in the desert places. Even in the midst of our pain, there is always room for rejoicing.

Most of us live with one goal in mind: we want to make it out of the desert! Yet God's leading into the desert is not accidental, nor is it incidental. It is meant for our good. He sets up breakthroughs for His children in the desert. Instead of focusing on escaping the desert, we should spend more time understanding how to thrive in the desert. We must learn to find joy in the wilderness.

📍 Read Exodus 14:15–28. Describe the miracle God gave the people of Israel.

 Why do you think God allowed all the Egyptians to die?

In the middle of the unexpected desert, what had looked like disaster for the people of Israel became the highlight of their lives so far. God literally separated the waters so His people could walk through the sea and safely away from their enemy. God delivered the people of Israel with a strong and mighty arm, and He did it for one reason only: His glory!

The people of Israel were astounded by this miracle of deliverance. They were flabbergasted. They were in awe. We're told that they *believed* God in that moment. I can't begin to imagine the joy they must have felt when they got to the other side of that water.

 Read Exodus 15:1–21. What was the response of the people of Israel to the miracle God had given them?

The desert had become a place of worship! Worship in song is one of the primary ways for us to declare the glory of God. Did you know that the song in Exodus 15 is the first song recorded in Scripture? It was later called "The Song of the Sea."

 Have you ever sung a "Song of the Sea" to God? To answer this question, you might need to think back to the last miracle God gave you. This might be a good place to stop and write a few lines to your own "Song of the Sea."

◉ Read Exodus 15:1–18 again and underline the words and phrases that declare the glory of God.

It's easy to sing about God's goodness and greatness when we've just walked through a parted Red Sea, isn't it? It's easy to declare God's goodness on the good days in life. Most of us, though, are fickle. We think God is good when life is good. But when life is hard, it's easy for us to question the goodness of God. It's easy to wonder about where God is and why His presence is missing.

Most of us misunderstand God's favor. We think of God's favor as His willingness to do what we want Him to do for us. While it's not wrong to sing praises to God on the good days, mature and believing faith in God's goodness learns to see past the good days to the steadfast faithfulness of God on every day of the week and in every season of life. We must learn to remember that God is good even on the bad days.

◉ Write down some of the ways God has shone His favor on you today.

◉ When was the last time you sang a song of praise to God? What if you were to start right now? Write down a few lines to express your praise to God, then sing those words out to Him in worship.

Modern-day Christians use the term *worship* to describe the singing part of our church experience. We tend to think of worship as something we do with a piano and a guitar, with a set of drums in the background. But singing is not the only way we worship God.

🔘 What are some other ways we can worship God?

Life is worship. Rejoicing in the Lord is worship. We must become people who learn to rejoice in God. The joy of the Lord *is* our strength. If you're like me, and you're much more accustomed to burdens than to praise and much more comfortable with suffering than with miracles, it's time for a change. Our suffering is often the soil through which miracles grow.

Sadly, our rejoicing, even when we do express it, never lasts long enough. No matter how many signs of God's favor we're given, we're always looking for more.

🔘 Read Exodus 15:22–24. How long did it take for the people of Israel to forget the power and goodness of God?

The people of Israel were fickle. Their faith was easily shaken. Their eyes were more focused on their circumstances than on their God. Their memories were short and their groanings loud.

We're not so different from the people of Israel.

Our suffering is often the soil through which miracles grow.

Every time I read about the people of Israel, I see myself in them. I am prone to worship when things are going my way. I am quick to praise God when life is good. But the minute I get a whiff of the arid wilderness, I revert to my true self: a grumbler, a doubter, a complainer. I'm not trying to confess my dirty laundry to you. I'm merely assessing my reality. Fortunately, God already knows how fickle we are.

Read Exodus 15:22–27 again. How did God respond to the grumbling of the people of Israel?

What does His response teach you about His faithfulness?

Remember that the story of the Bible is the story of God and His faithfulness to His people despite their continued disobedience. It's a story much less about us and much more about Him.

Your maturity in Christ is in direct proportion to your ability to sing songs of praise to God in the desert places of your life. One of the goals of the Christian walk is to become people who can glorify God and sing praises to Him—even in the wilderness.

Let's Make This Personal

📍 What was your reaction to reading Exodus 15:22–24?

📍 Do you identify with the people of Israel, or were you irritated with them?

📍 What have you learned so far about God's purpose for you in the desert places of your life?

📍 Think about your life. What triggers your grumbling?

📍 In which areas of your life have you been tempted to grumble?

Today's Take Home Point

While God's goodness is more easily seen
after the miracle, His goodness is real in
every season and in every outcome.

Final Thought

📍 Where in your life right now is God inviting you to start singing praises to Him?

Day 5: Forever Faithful

Reading: Exodus 16

Theme: God's presence is the food we need to satisfy our deepest longing.

I started my Christian walk in my teen years. I had no idea how things would play out. I thought life in Christ would be easy. I thought that because I had given my life to Jesus, everything else in life would flow smoothly. I've come to learn that life as a Christian is challenging. There are dry and dreary seasons. There are trials and temptations. There are detours and delays. I'm learning that these desert places are part of God's plan for me. It's in these desert places that God's faithfulness is most palpable.

> Let's read Exodus 16 today. Does it surprise you to find the people of Israel complaining again?

> Focus on verse 3. What can you conclude about the people of Israel's view of God here? Have you ever been tempted to doubt God's goodness too?

> Knowing what we have learned about God so far, was it likely that God had led the people of Israel this far only to let them die of hunger?

◉ Complaining isn't just an Old Testament problem. Read Philippians 2:14–16. According to Paul, how does complaining reflect on your Christian character?

God's response to Israel's complaining is astounding. Instead of punishing them for their persistent knuckleheadedness, He resolved their problem! He provided manna for them.

◉ Are you surprised that God extended more grace to the people of Israel despite their accusations?

◉ Describe the provision of manna that God gave to His people.

◉ How many days would there be food?

◉ What happened on the Sabbath?

📍 What were the people of Israel supposed to remember each time they gathered manna?

📍 Read Exodus 16:27. Why do you think the people of Israel went out on the Sabbath looking for manna despite God giving them specific instructions not to?

Manna became a sign of God's faithfulness for the people of Israel in the Old Testament. Day after day through the wilderness, God provided food for them. Night after night, the people slept with the assurance that God would have a meal prepared for them in the morning. Their persistent unfaithfulness didn't cause God's provision to stop.

📍 Read Exodus 16:35 and Joshua 5:12. When did the manna finally stop appearing?

📍 Why do you think that was?

For forty years, God displayed His faithfulness to His people through His daily bread for them. Although we no longer eat manna, God continues to reveal His faithfulness to us today through His daily provision for us.

◆ Read Deuteronomy 8:3. What do you learn about God's purpose for manna here?

◆ Read Matthew 4:4. Jesus quotes Deuteronomy 8:3. What bread is Jesus referring to here?

◆ Read Matthew 6:11. Jesus mentions daily bread in what is today known as the Lord's Prayer. What is Jesus asking His Father for here?

◆ Finally, read John 6:32–35. Who are we told can alone satisfy our deepest hunger?

God's greatest provision for His people is the gift of Himself. While most of us have an easier time thanking God for the gift of a sandwich, it's Jesus who is our most precious treasure. Whether you're stuck in a cycle of complaining or making your way out of the wilderness, Christ's presence in you and with you is all the food you need to make it through the day.

Forever faithful. The same God who invited Abraham into the actual desert, delivered Israel from the spiritual desert of Egypt, and led His people through forty years of the desert is still leading you today. Though God's desire is to see us grow in our willingness to trust Him, His faithfulness does not depend on how well we do that.

It has taken me a lifetime to understand that God's faithfulness is not proportionate to my performance. Faithful is who God is. Isn't it time we started believing Him?

Let's Make This Personal

📍 What are you most hungry for in this season of your life?

📍 How well are you feeding on God's Word for your nourishment?

📍 Would you say you're spiritually healthy or more on the anemic side?

◉ Where is there room to grow?

◉ Are you living in awareness of God's presence in your life right now? What are some ways you can live with a greater awareness of your spiritual reality?

Today's Take Home Point

The opportunities to glorify God, to rid ourselves of our fears, to satisfy our longings, and to deepen our experience of His goodness are just some of the gifts that God gives us through our desert places.

Final Thought

◉ What might God be inviting you to feed on in your soul's deepest hunger and longings?

Praying through Scripture—Week 2
Song in the Desert
Exodus 14:30–15:2, 19–21

Thus the LORD saved Israel that day from the hand of the Egyptians, and Israel saw the Egyptians dead on the seashore. Israel saw the great power that the LORD used against the Egyptians, so the people feared the LORD, and they believed in the LORD and in his servant Moses.

Then Moses and the people of Israel sang this song to the LORD, saying,

"I will sing to the LORD, for he has triumphed gloriously;
    the horse and his rider he has thrown into the sea.
The LORD is my strength and my song,
    and he has become my salvation;
this is my God, and I will praise him,
    my father's God, and I will exalt him...."

For when the horses of Pharaoh with his chariots and his horsemen went into the sea, the LORD brought back the waters of the sea upon them, but the people of Israel walked on dry ground in the midst of the sea. Then Miriam the prophetess, the sister of Aaron, took a tambourine in her hand, and all the women went out after her with tambourines and dancing. And Miriam sang to them:

"Sing to the LORD, for he has triumphed gloriously;
    the horse and his rider he has thrown into the sea."

Read the passage out loud once.

Now close your eyes and take a few deep breaths. Pray with me: "O God, I pray that You will help me to hear You speak during this time of meditation on Your Word. I open my hands to You. I open my ears to You."

Pause for eight to ten seconds.

Imagine you're one of the people of Israel. You've just walked across the Red Sea and still can't believe your eyes. Right before your very eyes the seas split open for you to walk through. Not a drop of water is on your clothes. Your friends are with you too. Think about the excitement on the other side of the Red Sea. Describe the look on people's faces. Think about the words being spoken all around you. Look back and describe the scene as the waters of the Red Sea cover the dry ground once again, killing with it Pharaoh's army and his horses. What comes to your mind as you think about God in this moment?

Read the passage again.

Pause for eight to ten seconds.

Now listen closely. Lean in a little more. You can tell Moses is speaking, but you're too far in the back to hear every word clearly. You're also too worked up with excitement to pay close attention. Oh, but wait, it sounds like someone just started to sing. You lean in and listen a bit more carefully. Indeed, it is a song you're hearing! Pretty soon everyone around you starts to sing the same song too. Some break out in dance.

Describe the scene. What is everybody excited about? What are you excited about? Are you dancing with everyone too?

Pause for five to eight seconds.

Is there a smile on your face yet? Think about God for a moment. Think about the last few weeks that have led up to this song. Remember how tired you were in Egypt? Remember how scared you were when you lived through the plagues? Did you ever think you'd be free to dance in the desert? Could you ever have imagined the things you've gone through the last few weeks? Think about how much your life has changed in the last weeks. What are some of the things you'd like to thank God for?

You look up and see Miriam interrupt the song. She has a tambourine in her hand. She looks majestic and unstoppable, radiant with joy. The women around her pick up her cue and join in singing this celebration of worship. You recognize several faces in the group. The women are dancing with pure joy. Their eyes are raised to the heavens, their voices loud and harmonious. They have no thought of what others are thinking about them. They're caught up in a song of praise so genuine it's almost too intimate to witness.

But wait … you can hardly believe it, but somewhere in the middle of the song, you jumped in and joined the chorus of praise! Your hands are lifted high. Your heart is so full it's about to burst. You take a deep breath. You feel the sun on your face.

Never in your life did you imagine life could be so good.

You say thank You. Over and over again, your lips move of their own accord, singing praise to God, saying thank You.

Pause for eight to ten seconds.

Can you feel the joy? In the midst of your desert, can you see the miracle of the parted Red Sea in your own life? In what ways have you been freed from slavery? Perhaps the desert is the place where God is extending you the invitation to dance for Him with all your might. Are you willing to do it?

Are you willing to ignore what other people think of your dance moves? Are you willing to sing a new song to God? You have reason to sing, even in your desert places. Are you willing to become even more undignified for the sake of your King?

Session 3

Purpose in the Desert

Exodus 13:17–22

Watch the session 3 video now. The video is available at DavidCCook.org/access, with access code DesertPlaces.

1. God will never lead you to a desert place that He does not intend to use ____ _____ _____.

2. God will never lead you to a desert place without also _____ ____ _____ through it.

3. God will always use your desert places to reveal what you _____ about His faithfulness.

4. God will always use your desert places to show you the _____ of His faithfulness to you.

Video Group Discussion Questions

After watching the video, discuss the following questions in your group.

📍 How does understanding that the desert is never an accident in God's economy change the way you perceive the desert in your life right now?

📍 Have you ever felt like you're wandering without direction in your Christian life? How has God directed you in the past in ways you did not expect?

📍 Consider your reaction to your present wilderness places. How are you reacting to the difficulties in your life? What do your reactions say regarding your beliefs about God?

📍 What are some of the practical ways you've experienced God's daily manna of faithfulness?

📍 When you think about how faithful God has been to you, what song of worship comes to your heart and mind?

Week 3: Mercy in the Desert

2 Timothy 2:13
"If we are faithless, he remains faithful."

Introduction

I was once pulled over by a police officer for speeding. I had just finished teaching at a women's conference, and I was in a hurry to get home. My friend Tina was with me. We were excited about all God had done at the conference and were having a great time laughing and telling stories.

I knew I was speeding but didn't expect to get caught. So I was quite annoyed when, twenty-five miles south of my home, police sirens suddenly brought me back to earth from my post-conference glow.

As the police officer made his way to my car, I thought of a million excuses I could give: I wasn't paying attention. Tina's jokes had distracted me from careful driving. I'm a doctor and needed to get back to my patients (that one usually works!). Instead, I sheepishly gave him my driver's license and said a quick prayer that my ticket would be merciful.

I waited, the weight of my guilt on my shoulders, while the police officer ruminated over my future. A few agonizing minutes later, the officer walked over to my car, handed me my driver's license, and told me he had decided to simply give me a warning.

Ah, mercy! It had never felt so good!

We've all been there. We know the feeling. We know our wrong. We know we deserve punishment. When God grants us mercy, it's too much. We don't always know what to do with His extravagant love.

Our lesson this week is about mercy: God's mercy to His people despite their wrongdoing. What God does in Jeremiah 31 is almost too good to be true.

I hope you're ready to be radically transformed by God's grace this week.

Day 1: Cycle of Failure

Reading: Jeremiah 1:1–10

Theme: It is God's goodness that awakens us to our need for change.

We're jumping from the book of Exodus all the way to Jeremiah this week. This may seem like a big leap, but it's not as hard as you might imagine to get up to speed on what happened to the people of Israel during this almost one-thousand-year span. It was basically a cycle of failure.

The exodus from Egypt happened around 1440 BC. We're now in the years 627–582 BC, in the book of Jeremiah. Although almost eight hundred years have passed, some cycles did not change. The people of Israel had spent the last few hundred years in defeat. They had established a pattern of disbelieving God despite His faithfulness to them. They repeatedly turned to idols instead of worshipping the living God. He would send prophets to warn Israel of incoming judgment, and the people would ignore the prophets until they felt the consequences of their sin. Then with their tail between their legs, the people would come crawling back to God with words of repentance. It took longer for their hearts to change.

Have you ever been stuck in a cycle of defeat? I have, and it's a hard place to live. Sometimes it takes a disaster to finally break that cycle of failure. That's what happened to the people of Israel.

Jeremiah's ministry started a little "out of the blue" when he was just a young man. Even though God had clearly called him to speak on His behalf (Jer. 1), Jeremiah was routinely rejected by his people and punished for speaking the truth. He warned the people of Israel that they would be defeated by the Babylonians and exiled to the Babylonian Empire. The people's response was to accuse him of being negative and judgmental. The more he prophesied, the more he was punished. He was ridiculed and mocked. He was accused of lying and treason. Yet every word he spoke did come to pass.

Do you identify more with Jeremiah or with the people of Israel? Are you a truth-teller hated by the culture, or are you stuck in a cycle unwilling to heed the warning God is sending your way?

◉ Read Jeremiah 2:13. What are the two things that God had against His people?

◉ What are some of the "broken cisterns" in our culture today? Why don't they satisfy the human heart?

It's only when we're willing to admit the depth of our brokenness that we become ready for God's healing and transformation. When we're willing to admit that, we become ready for God's healing and transformation. Before we get to Jeremiah 31 and give our attention to God's mercy toward His people, let's spend time today understanding the depth of brokenness and need that the people of Israel were in. We will do so by making a few pit stops in the following verses:

◉ Read Jeremiah 3:6–14. How many times does God accuse His people of being faithless and treacherous?

◉ Read Jeremiah 4:1–4. What was God's plea to Israel?

◉ Read Jeremiah 4:22. In what ways do the people of Israel remind you of the culture we're living in today?

◉ Read Jeremiah 13:23–25. What was at the heart of Israel's sin?

◉ In what ways have you forgotten God and trusted in lies?

Things were not going well for the people of Israel. They were stuck in a cycle of defeat and rebellion. No amount of preaching was making a difference. This is a dangerous place to live. Sadly, it's a familiar place for many of us. We know to do right, but we simply choose not to. In Jeremiah 25, God's wrath is at a tipping point. It's time for judgment to come to the house of God.

◉ Read Jeremiah 25:3. What are the areas in your life right now where you know the right thing to do but are still willfully choosing not to listen to God?

Some passages of Scripture are harder to hear than others. Most of the book of Jeremiah fits into that category. The problem with living in a place of persistent defeat is that we become accustomed to that place. Like a pig in a pigsty, eventually we stop noticing the horrid smell.

It's only when we're willing to admit the depth of our brokenness that we become ready for God's healing and transformation.

Have you ever stayed at a really nasty motel? I have. And yet, I adjusted. What made me cringe when I checked in began to feel like home after just a few minutes. Sin is like that—shocking to step into but surprisingly comfortable after a while.

Sometimes, even when we want to leave a cycle of defeat, it's hard to do it. Over time, we stop believing that change is possible. We resolve to change—and then we fail so often that it becomes easier to give up hope than to try to convince ourselves and God that we're serious about changing this time.

The desert of our own failure is one of the hardest deserts to be stuck in. As long as we can blame our failures and sins on someone else, we can hold on to the notion that we might still be worthy of redemption.

Yet true change is impossible until we are willing to admit that we are the problem. When we stop blaming others and own our own sin, we take the first step toward freedom. We call this the process of repentance.

But how? What's the tipping point to move us from the pigsty to the presence of the Father? The people of Israel offer a wonderful illustration of the process.

As we dig into this week's study in Jeremiah 31, we're going to better understand the catalyst that led the people of Israel out of their cycle of defeat. We will learn that it wasn't their guilt that God used to motivate His people to change. It wasn't fear of punishment that did the trick, although avoiding bad consequences did work for them in the short run. What God used to propel His people back to Himself was something a whole lot better than guilt and punishment. We will cover this tomorrow, but until then, here's something to get you thinking.

◉ Read Romans 2:4. According to Paul, what is it that makes us want to change?

We've made a big transition this week from the book of Exodus to the pre-exile era in the history of God's people. As we allow this foundational information from today's lesson to settle in, let's spend some time making things more personal.

Let's Make This Personal

Spend some time in reflection and prayer before answering these questions.

◉ Where in my life am I stuck in a cycle of defeat and shame?

◉ How many times have I tried to convince God that I really want to change?

◉ Why have I chosen the pain of sin over the goodness of God even when I know how bad it feels to continue to live in sin?

⦿ Do I really believe God can help me out of this cycle of sin?

⦿ Do I really want to change? What price am I willing to pay for change to take place in me?

These are hard questions. They will take time to answer honestly. The truth is that you can't promise your way out of your failure and defeat. You can't work your way out of your mess. You can't hope your way out of your cycle of failure and defeat.

Only God can pull you out of it.

The question is: Do you believe Him?

Today's Take Home Point

Brokenness is God's invitation for you to change.

Final Thought

⦿ What is God's invitation for you in your places of brokenness?

Day 2: *Surprised by Love*

Reading: Jeremiah 31:1–17

Theme: It's the extravagant love of God that tips the scales toward change.

So where do we fit into the scope of God's promises? Where does our story fit into God's greater story?

We've been focused on God's dealings with His people, the people of Israel. But what about us? What part of God's promise to Abraham applies to Christians? While it may be fun watching someone else open a beautiful gift, that joy can take you only so far. Eventually, it's easy to feel a little bit left out. But God's love doesn't stop with Abraham, and it's not limited to Abraham's descendants. It's extended to every one of us who is seeking to belong today and forevermore.

When we started this series, we spent time in Genesis 12:1–3, the promise God gave to Abraham. We learned the three elements of the promise that propelled Abraham out of his comfort zone and into the unknown future. While Abraham was promised a son, God's promise to Abraham extended well past the birth of Isaac. Let me show you how.

📍 Read Galatians 3:16. Cross-reference Genesis 15:5 and Genesis 18:1–8. What connection can you make between the son God promised to Abraham and the coming Messiah?

Remember that the story of the Bible is the story of God. It's a story of redemption through the birth of a Savior whose name is Jesus. While it may feel like we're covering a lot of ground in this study, what we're really doing is learning to see God's hand in the story of humanity. And it all goes back to Jesus. All the way from the book of Genesis and on into the wilderness where the people of Israel fed on daily manna, the picture of the Messiah in the Old Testament stands boldly pointing toward the coming birth of Jesus Christ. It's *this* story that hugely affects your life and mine today!

God didn't just promise Abraham a son. God also promised Abraham the birth of Jesus through his seed in order to save us from our sin. But how do we jump from Abraham to Jesus? Jeremiah 31 is a watershed chapter in the Old Testament that will help us make that leap. This week's reading will land us smack-dab in the middle of God's astounding mercy and unfathomable grace.

📍 Read Jeremiah 31. It's long but worth your time to read it. If you do nothing else in today's homework, simply jot down one or two of your favorite verses from this chapter here.

We spent time yesterday getting a feel for the rebellion of the people of Israel despite all that God had done for them. They refused to believe God even after He gave them many opportunities to trust Him. They repeatedly turned to their own foolish ways. They forfeited their peace and security because they couldn't clearly see just how good God is.

After all the ways the people of Israel neglected God, the prophecy that they would be taken into exile and ruled by the Babylonian Empire is hardly a surprise. If anything, it's surprising that their punishment was limited to only a seventy-year exile.

But God's ways are not like our ways, and His thoughts are not like our thoughts—and that's the best news in the world for us today.

📍 Read Jeremiah 31:1–5. How does God respond to Israel's unfaithfulness?

Jeremiah 31 is a fascinating passage of Scripture, but it can be a little difficult to understand. Unlike the writings of other prophets like Ezekiel, the content of Jeremiah's writings is not meant to be strictly chronological. Instead, the content covers two themes that intersect in Jeremiah 31:31–35. On the one hand is God's persistent faithfulness to His people Israel. This faithfulness rested on God's unconditional covenant to Abraham. On the other hand is God's future promise for all of us.

I'm talking about the New Covenant, which is revisited in Jeremiah 31:31–35. I'm talking about Jesus.

◉ Read Hebrews 8:6–13. What makes this New Covenant so different from the Old?

◉ Read Hebrews 7:22–28. On what basis does God hinge His New Covenant to His people?

◉ What do you think God's motivation is in offering Jesus to be the mediator of the New Covenant?

If you miss the *why* of Jesus, you might miss everything. There is a reason Jeremiah 31 is our text for this week. In the middle of a passage focused on judgment and impending doom, Jeremiah transitions into a message of hope and a future.

◉ Read Jeremiah 31:1–5 again. What emotion motivates God to go after Israel in the middle of their wilderness?

Love. It turns out that all we need is indeed just love. It was love that motivated the heart of God to find His people in the wilderness. It was love that moved God to give Abraham the promise of a son who would redeem His people from their sin. It is God's love that moves us to repentance, and it is God's love that beckons us to Him today.

God's faithfulness to His people is best understood in light of His perfect and unconditional love for us.

◉ Are you surprised by God's love for the people of Israel? Are you relieved by it? What emotions flood your soul as you consider how, instead of giving the people of Israel a well-deserved punishment, He merely beckons them back to Him with His love?

Jeremiah's message was an avalanche of grace in a time of great heaviness. It was a message of mercy that continues to flow over us today. His prophecy regarding the New Covenant was life-changing.

◉ Read Galatians 3:23–4:6. What made the New Covenant so radical?

God's faithfulness is best seen in the person of Jesus Christ. Without Christ, there is no life. Without Christ, we have no hope. Without Christ, we remain stuck in a cycle of failure and defeat. And the way out of our desert places is not our own effort or performance, it's not our own past track record, and it's not our wishful thinking. The way out of our desert places is God's unconditional and never-changing love for His people.

While the promise for a son came to Abraham, the promise of *the* Son comes to you and me today.

Let's Make This Personal

How have you experienced God's love for you in the wilderness?

Where in your life are you still trying to impress God with your works? How does understanding how much God loves you motivate you to want to change?

Repentance is simply our acknowledgment of our sinfulness in light of God's holiness. It's our way of surrendering to God's love. It's our awakening to the reality that even though we don't deserve God's love, it's ours for the taking, simply because of God's grace. Repentance is not a onetime action but a daily surrender and rejoicing in this unconditional, unstoppable love of God for you and me.

You can check your level of understanding of God's love for you by the amount of repentance you're living in.

Today's Take Home Point

The more you believe God loves you,
the easier it is for you to repent.

Final Thought

What's God's invitation to you as He awakens you to His never-ending love?

Day 3: Second Chances

Reading: Hebrews 10:1–18

Theme: Jesus is the reason we are freed from the burden of performance.

I've always connected with the prophet Jeremiah. He's like the Eeyore of Old Testament prophets. He's also known as the weeping prophet. He did not have an easy or successful life. Most of his prophecies were warnings of upcoming disasters. He was rejected by his peers and threatened by his superiors.

Admittedly, Jeremiah spoke some pretty harsh truths to the people of Israel, but his warnings were not unfamiliar to them, nor were they surprising. For centuries, God had lined up priests and prophets to plead with the people of Israel and warn them of their need to clean up their act. But over and over again, the people of Israel ignored His warnings.

Yet as hard as Jeremiah's message was, he also wrote some of the most memorable verses in all of Scripture. For example, Jeremiah wrote, "Your words were found, and I ate them, and your words became to me a joy and the delight of my heart" (Jer. 15:16). He also wrote: "For I know the plans I have for you, declares the LORD, plans for welfare and not for evil, to give you a future and a hope" (Jer. 29:11). Jeremiah's message of repentance was not one of doom. It was a message of hope.

It was a message of second chances.

God, you see, is a God of second chances. He's always near when we turn to Him for help. If you're feeling the weight of your bad decisions, you're going to love today's lesson.

📍 Read Jeremiah 31:1–5. What word is repeated over and over in this passage?

I love the word *again*. Some days, I wonder if I've pushed God too far. Some days, I wonder if this time I've crossed a line of God's mercy. The longer I live as a Christian, the more aware I am of my persistent ability to sin. I tell myself that I should know better by now. I berate myself after promising to change a million times and yet still failing in the same old ways. I want to believe that God will remain faithful to me. But truthfully, some days, I wonder if I'll be the exception to His rule: What if I'm beyond redemption?

The God we meet in Jeremiah 31 defies our doubt and fear. He loves us again and again and again. His willingness to offer us a second chance is astounding.

♀ Where in your life do you need a second chance?

One of the biggest differences between the Old and New Testaments is in how we relate to God. The Old Testament presents our relationship with God in terms of the law.

♀ Read Deuteronomy 11:26–28. What did God's blessing hinge upon before Jesus?

♀ Read Matthew 6:33. What does God's blessing in the New Testament hinge upon?

Despite the fact that the law was impossible to obey perfectly, the people knew that God's blessing on their lives hinged on whether they would keep God's commandments or not. Every year, the high priest offered a sacrifice on behalf of the people to atone for their sins.

Every year, the people were reminded of their inability to keep God's commands and their desperate need for God's mercy.

In the New Testament, everything changed. Jesus became the perfect Lamb of God who would once and for all pay the price for our sin. The shedding of His blood on the cross was the perfect atonement for us forevermore.

◉ Read Hebrews 10:1–18. What are some of the differences between the Old Testament sacrifices of bulls and goats and the New Testament sacrifice of Jesus?

◉ If you keep in mind the Old Testament mindset of blessing that hinged upon obedience, the language of Jeremiah 31 becomes even more astounding. How do you think the people of Israel responded to the language of Jeremiah 31?

I've noticed a pattern in my life: even though I intellectually understand God's faithfulness to His people, I find it hard to trust that He is consistently good to me. It's easy for me to revert to a contractual relationship with Him, in which I act as if He will bless me more if I'm more obedient to Him. I'm a New Testament believer stuck in Old Testament habits and ways.

But we've been given so much more in Christ! We've been given unfathomable grace in Him.

Because of Jesus, God's goodness is not contingent on my obedience but on Christ's obedience on my behalf. Because of Jesus, my sins are forgiven, and I'm set free from the compulsion to come to God based on my perfect performance. Jesus is not our reward for good behavior but the motivation for it. Spend some time in Ephesians 2:8–9 if you need God's word on the matter.

It's easy for me to revert to a contractual relationship with God, in which I act as if He will bless me more if I'm more obedient to Him.

I mentioned earlier that Jeremiah reminded me of Eeyore, but that might not be so true. It wasn't negativity that drove Jeremiah to speak a difficult message—it was brokenness. Jeremiah's tears were born out of brokenness for God's people. Jeremiah understood God's love and mercy so well that his heart broke over their perpetual refusal to turn to their loving and merciful Father. Jeremiah's heart overflowed with sorrow for his people, who missed God's extravagant love for them. The same guy who wrote Jeremiah 31 is the guy who wrote Lamentations 3.

Read Lamentations 3:17–24. What attributes of God further magnify His willingness to give us second chances?

New mercies every morning. Steadfast love that never ceases. That's the good news of the gospel: our God is a God of second chances. Not one of us is beyond His redemption. You can't out-sin God's love. Our culture can't outgrow God's love. The church can't outsmart God's love.

Some days, our world feels too broken. It's easy to lose hope. It's easy to point out the many ways we have become unfaithful to God. If there ever were a people who deserved to give up, it should have been the people of Israel. If there ever were a people who deserved to be judged, it was the people of Israel. But instead of correcting them with words of condemnation, Jeremiah 31 is God's love letter to His wayward people. Through the offering of the New Covenant, God offered Himself afresh to His people. It took over four hundred years for them to believe it—and even then, almost everyone still missed it!

The magnificence of the New Covenant is that, once and for all, God extends a second chance to you today, because Jesus was willing to pay the price for your sin. You are forgiven because He was forsaken. You're accepted because Jesus was condemned. You're alive and well, and His Spirit is within you because He died and rose again.[9]

Today, you and I have been given a second chance, and it's all because of Jesus and His unconditional love for us. No wonder we call it amazing love. No wonder we stand in awe when we think about His love.

Let's Make This Personal

📍 Have you ever found yourself in a place where you doubt God's willingness to give you a second chance? Where in your life do you feel you deserve God's punishment?

📍 What do you feel when you consider that God is willing to give you a second chance in the place where you fear you've already run out of chances?

📍 What do you see and feel when you look at the people living in your culture? How does today's lesson encourage you to go on in a faithless culture?

Today's Take Home Point

God's faithfulness to us does not
depend on our faithfulness to Him.

Final Thought

What's God's invitation to you through today's teaching?

Day 4: Future Hope
Reading: Jeremiah 31
Theme: We have hope in our desert places because of what's still to come.

When I graduated from medical school, I was given a long white coat and a name badge that said I was a doctor. I started my residency in pediatrics and was expected to see patients on my own and to treat them appropriately. I introduced myself as a doctor to my patients, and I acted like a doctor, but I was still far from feeling like a doctor.

I had an attending physician to whom I reported. I did not make one decision on my own without the attending physician guiding the process—and thank God for that! On some days, I encountered my attending physician once a day, while other times, we met multiple times a day. On some days, the attending physician corrected my diagnostic acumen, while on other days, I was commended for a job well done.

During those three years of my residency, I was a doctor but not yet a doctor.

There is a tension in Jeremiah 31 that feels a little bit like that. It's the reality of living in both the here and now and the not yet. We should be familiar with the chapter by now. Like me, you might love the words of Jeremiah 31 but also be a little confused.

As a New Testament believer, I've experienced God's abiding presence and blessing in my life in a way that wasn't yet known in the Old Testament. The prophetic words of Jeremiah 31:31–34 make more sense to me each time I read them. The reality of the New Covenant shines in our lives each time we bow our heads and pray. We know intimacy with God in a way that our forefathers did not. Jesus Christ is alive in us. The Holy Spirit is our present reality even on our most challenging days.

Yet most of us still yearn for more. Our hearts are still restless and hunger for more. We want to experience God more tangibly. We long to hear His voice and be with Him. We want to see Jesus. We forget what Philip forgot in John 14:8–9. When Philip asked Jesus, "Lord, show us the Father, and it is enough for us," Jesus answered, "Have I been with you so long, and you still do not know me, Philip?" We already have what and who we long for.

While we can experience God much more intimately than the people of Israel could in the Old Testament, we are still living in the here and now but not yet. Someday, we will experience God more fully. Jeremiah 31 alludes to that day. I can't wait.

Like my days in residency, we are already fully with Christ but not yet fully with Christ. We live in the tension of the here and now but not yet, and no Scripture passage depicts it better than Jeremiah 31.

♀ Read Jeremiah 31 one more time. What are some of the promises that are yet to come for God's people?

♀ The trouble with living in the "not yet" is that it's easy to lose hope. It's easy to drift into the Slough of Despond. Read Jeremiah 31:10–17. What are some of the ways that God offers hope in our despair?

We lose hope for a lot of reasons. We have unmet expectations and unexpected failures. We have unexpected disappointments and are stuck in unloving relationships. We have unrequited love and unwelcome consequences. Yet without hope, the Christian life is impossible. Everything we believe rests on hope. We've got to learn to hang on to hope in the desert places of our lives.

♀ Read Jeremiah 31:17. What is the hope for our future referred to here?

Hope is the confidence that God is able to intervene in our situation in miraculous ways but may not choose to do so. When the days get long and our responsibilities too weighty, we must learn to embrace the things God has promised us: that He will never leave us nor forsake us (Heb. 13:5), that all things will work out for our good (Rom. 8:28), and that there is a reward for our perseverance (James 5:10–11).

Jeremiah 31 is God's gift of hope to us when we're stuck in desert places. It's a reminder that we were created for more. While God showers us with blessings here in this lifetime, Jeremiah 31 is a reminder that this life is not the end of our story. There's still more to come.

Perhaps no verse is able to move us from the burden of introspection and despondency faster than Jeremiah 31:25.

📍 Read Jeremiah 31:25. What does God promise will replenish us when we're weary?

Despite the good news that Jeremiah shared with the people of Israel in Jeremiah 31, they still rejected the message God was offering them. They never fully received God's love. They were ultimately defeated by the Babylonian Empire and taken into captivity.

📍 Why do you think the people of Israel refused God's message of love?

When all is said and done, perhaps it's the desert that awakens us to our need for God. The people of Israel did eventually rebuild Jerusalem under the leadership of Nehemiah, but their true redemption wasn't completed until the coming of Jesus. Don't worry. We'll get there in our study next week.

> When all is said and done, perhaps it's the desert that awakens us to our need for God.

I remember the first time I was called to the bedside of a dying infant at 3:00 a.m. The little baby was burning up with fever and needed help. My first instinct was to look around for a doctor. *Someone help this child!* I thought. The nurse at the bedside looked me straight in the eyes and asked: "Doctor, give me the orders for this child. What do you want me to do?" In that moment, I woke up to who I was. I knew exactly what to do. And by God's grace, the baby survived!

I was becoming a doctor.

You and I are in the process of becoming more complete in Christ. The moment we receive Christ, He comes to live in us. We become fully *with* Him, yet we are not fully with Christ yet. The hope we have today is in the perfect love of Christ for us in the dryness of our desert places. That hope is both here and not yet. It's a present hope, because we have Christ with us now, but it's also a future hope, because someday we will be with Him forever.

♀ In Jeremiah 31:22, the prophet asks, "How long will you waver, O faithless daughter?" As we complete our time together today, how would you answer that question?

Let's Make This Personal

♀ What are some of the aspects of your Christian life that have led you to lose hope as you wait for Christ's future reign?

📍 How does God's presence with you satisfy you completely right now?

📍 List some practical ways you've experienced satisfaction in Christ so far in your Christian life.

Today's Take Home Point

In Christ, we have everything we need right now—and yet there is still more to come.

Final Thought

📍 What's God's invitation to you as you live in the tension between the here and now and the not yet?

Day 5: Unshakable Joy

Reading: Jeremiah 31:4–17

Theme: There is always reason to rejoice in the desert places.

I don't laugh nearly as much as I should. It didn't always used to be this way. But somewhere in the desert places in my life, I became more accustomed to frowning in worry than laughing in joy. I forgot that joy is my inheritance as a Christian and follower of Jesus Christ.

We're more than halfway into our study on God's faithfulness to His people through desert places. We started our journey with Abraham all the way back in Genesis, then moved along to the exodus of God's people from the bondage of Egypt, and now we have landed in the life of God's people pre-exile. Throughout our trek so far, we've deepened our knowledge of God's character and His commitment to us.

One of the highlights of this week's study is Jeremiah 31, an amazing chapter of Scripture. The people of Israel were walking through a cultural desert. No one seemed interested in God and His ways. Immorality was at an all-time high, and humility was at an all-time low. Yet in the middle of a culture full of brokenness and godlessness, God faithfully offered the gift of mercy for His people.

Our culture is not so different today. Everywhere we look, we're surrounded by brokenness and godlessness. Even the church is hurting. It's hard to sense the joy of the Lord in a season of darkness, let alone see revival coming. Some seasons make it difficult to believe that better days are on the way. Yet, according to Jeremiah 31, better times are indeed coming! Our time in God's Word today is intended to bring us back to a place of joy, no matter how barren our present desert season feels.

♥ Read Jeremiah 31:4–17. Underline every word or phrase that points to joy. What are some of the reasons the people of Israel were given to rejoice about?

How would you rate your joy meter in your desert place right now?

Though the words of Jeremiah 31 were written thousands of years ago for the people of Israel, in what ways do they speak to your heart today?

The people of Israel were in a mess. Political instability was prevalent. There was a takeover by the Babylonian Empire on the way. There was turmoil between both parts of their own divided kingdom. The covenant that God had made to Abraham seemed long forgotten. God Himself seemed like a faded memory or background noise, at best. Yet in the midst of this chaos, God promised His people joy in their future. This joy did not depend on their own goodness and efforts but on God's covenant to His people. Joy was indeed the legacy of the people of Israel.

Let's go back to Genesis 21:1–6. What was the reason that Abraham and Sarah rejoiced?

Abraham and Sarah had waited twenty-five years for their son, Isaac, to be born. By the time just before Sarah conceived, everyone had given up hope that God would fulfill His promise to Abraham. Even Abraham's faith was hanging by a thread. Yet Abraham and Sarah were about to learn that in the desert places of their waiting, God's word had not failed them. His promises had not faltered. What He said, He did. Abraham and Sarah could hardly believe their eyes. When their eyes landed on their bundle of joy, Sarah named the long-awaited son Isaac, meaning "laugher." The very naming of Isaac became an act of worship and rejoicing.

For Abraham, it was the birth of a son that brought joy. In Jeremiah 31, it's the promise of the redemption of Israel that was meant to bring joy—even when the people of Israel still did not fully comprehend it.

⦿ Check out Jeremiah 31:27, 31, and 38. The phrase "Behold, the days are coming" appears three times. What days might the prophet be referring to?

I love the duality of Jeremiah 31. On the one hand, God's word of promise is to Israel in that era, prophesying their own future as a nation. On the other hand, it is God's word of promise to us, His people today, as we consider what's still to come. While our joy became complete with the advent of Jesus, mediator of the New Covenant, part of the promise of Jeremiah 31 is still yet to come. This entire chapter is a prophecy of our lives in the new millennium. One day, we will experience unhindered joy with the Lord.

In the meantime, we have Jesus, who is the reason for our rejoicing right now.

If you're stuck in a desert season, you can know intellectually that Jesus is good news but still find it hard to feel joy. I get it. I live in the cup-half-empty world. But we don't have to stay there. Read the following verses as an exercise in meditating on some of the ways God has faithfully made provision for our joy right now.

Jeremiah 15:16

Psalm 100:1–2

Galatians 5:22

Philippians 4:4–6

James 1:2–3

Romans 15:13

There is reason for joy no matter how dry our desert places are. Most of us understand that we *should* rejoice no matter what. We just have a hard time doing it. We witnessed that pattern in week 2 of our study. When the people of Israel crossed the bottom of the Red Sea, they sure felt happy. It was easy to rejoice over the goodness of the Lord in the aftermath of that miracle. It's in the desert places of our lives where we must learn to see the goodness of God. It's in our barrenness that we must by faith believe that our God is faithful no matter what.

While Exodus 15 is a song of worship in answer to prayer, Jeremiah 31 is the song we must learn to sing even when our prayers remain unanswered and our present circumstances seem unchanged. Jeremiah 31 is the song of God's people whose hope is fully resting on the faithfulness and goodness of God.

♦ When it comes to singing praise to God, are you more familiar with the song of Exodus 15 or the song of Jeremiah 31?

Joy does not hinge on us developing a problem-free life. Joy is ours today, regardless of our circumstances. God's mercy is best seen by His gift of unshakable joy to us, even in our desert places.

Let's Make This Personal

♦ Where in your life are you lacking joy?

⦿ What are you still waiting for to experience joy in the Lord? What are practical ways you can express joy today?

Today's Take Home Point

Learning to laugh in your desert places is
an act of faith in the goodness of God.

Final Thought

⦿ What is God's invitation to you when it comes to learning to rejoice in your present painful circumstances?

Praying through Scripture—Week 3

Mourning to Joy

Jeremiah 30:1–4, 8–11; 31:1–3

The word that came to Jeremiah from the LORD: "Thus says the LORD, the God of Israel: Write in a book all the words that I have spoken to you. For behold, days are coming, declares the LORD, when I will restore the fortunes of my people, Israel and Judah, says the LORD, and I will bring them back to the land that I gave to their fathers, and they shall take possession of it."

These are the words that the LORD spoke concerning Israel and Judah: …

"And it shall come to pass in that day, declares the LORD of hosts, that I will break his yoke from off your neck, and I will burst your bonds, and foreigners shall no more make a servant of him. But they shall serve the LORD their God and David their king, whom I will raise up for them.

'Then fear not, O Jacob my servant, declares the LORD,
    nor be dismayed, O Israel;
for behold, I will save you from far away,
    and your offspring from the land of their captivity.
Jacob shall return and have quiet and ease,
    and none shall make him afraid.
For I am with you to save you, declares the LORD;
I will make a full end of all the nations
    among whom I scattered you,
    but of you I will not make a full end.
I will discipline you in just measure,
    and I will by no means leave you unpunished.'" …

"At that time, declares the LORD, I will be the God of all the clans of Israel, and they shall be my people."

Thus says the LORD:

"The people who survived the sword
  found grace in the wilderness;
when Israel sought for rest,
  the LORD appeared to him from far away.
I have loved you with an everlasting love;
  therefore I have continued my faithfulness to you."

Read the passage out loud once.

Now close your eyes and take a few deep breaths. Pray with me: "O God, I pray that You will help me to hear You speak during this time of meditation on Your Word. I open my hands to You. I open my ears to You."

Pause for eight to ten seconds.

Imagine you're one of the scribe's helpers who has been called to work with Jeremiah. You've heard of Jeremiah by reputation. You know him to be a prophet, but you also know he's been persecuted for the tough prophecies he's spoken. You know he was almost nearly killed for speaking judgment over the people of Israel. In fact, everyone in town is talking about Jeremiah's prediction of an upcoming captivity. Your friends and family heard that you were invited to help Jeremiah. You were warned about him. You were told to watch your back. But you couldn't help yourself. Deep in your gut, something tells you Jeremiah is speaking the truth.

You've noticed that Jeremiah doesn't say much, but you catch him often wiping tears from his eyes. You've caught him on his knees, head bowed low, listening. Today, he calls you over and tells you to start writing. He's received a message from God.

You expect a message of doom. You expect judgment. You expect words of revenge and anger over sin. But as you start writing the words that Jeremiah is dictating, you look up. You can hardly believe your ears.

Read the passage again.

Pause for eight to ten seconds.

What goes through your mind as you listen to the love letter God is giving to your people? What emotions fill your heart as you read the words you've just penned? You think about the state of affairs in your world. If you're being honest, you can't blame Jeremiah for his rebuke of your people. They deserve punishment. Their actions reflect a disdain of God. Their homes are filled with false gods that have not satisfied. You think about your own family. Instead of centering their lives around God and His ways, it's worldly comfort everyone is seeking: Money. Sex. Power. More. It's as if God's Word has been forgotten, or worse yet, ridiculed. You can't help it. You feel guilty for the many ways you've broken God's laws.

But instead of punishment, God speaks words that are hard to believe. They sound like someone in love. They sound as if God is desperately longing for the hearts of His people.

Read the passage again.

Pause for eight to ten seconds.

What moves your heart to tears as you reflect on God's love for you? What do you long to do in response to this love letter you've been given?

You look up and notice Jeremiah is waiting to dictate more of the letter. Except this time, you swear you can see the shadow of a smile on his face.

Session 4

Mercy in the Desert

Jeremiah 31:2-14

Watch the session 4 video now. The video is available at DavidCCook.org/access, with access code DesertPlaces.

1. When I get stuck in a cycle of failure, it's important to remember that I'm never outside the reach of _____ _____.

2. When I get stuck in a cycle of exhaustion, it's important to remember that it's not my _____ but God's that save me.

3. When I get stuck in a cycle of broken promises to God, it's important to remember that it's not _____ to God but His promises to me that sustain me.

4. When I get stuck in a cycle of despair, it's important to remember God's unflinching _____ to my joy.

Video Group Discussion Questions

After watching the video, discuss the following questions in your group.

♀ Have you ever felt outside the reach of God's love? What led you to feel that way?

♀ Think of the ways that you try to perform your way back into God's favor. When do you find yourself most prone to do so?

♀ Take some time and review some of the promises that God has made to you as His follower. Share one or two of the most meaningful ones with your group.

♀ When was the last time you felt joy as a Christian? How has Jeremiah 31 refocused your eyes on the truth of who God is and the gift of joy you've been given?

♀ What was your favorite verse in Jeremiah 31? Share the reason with your group.

Week 4: The Gift of Desert Places

1 Thessalonians 5:24
"He who calls you is faithful; he will surely do it."

Introduction

You've probably picked up by now, especially if you've been watching the videos, that my pace is divided between fast and faster. I move quickly. I talk fast because I think fast. I think fast, therefore I move fast. If you're wired like me, you're probably reveling in finally finding a Bible study that can keep up with your pace. If you're not wired like me, I'm glad you're still here.

Whether you're an introvert or an extrovert, a fast mover or in slow motion, most of us can agree on one thing: we hate to wait! We are wired to want quickly in a life that demands we wait. Our culture has not helped our plight of impatience. We're trained to hurry up, whether it's through on-demand movies, Amazon Prime, or instant access to both meals and medical care. I wonder if we've been ruined for the normal Christian life.

The Christian life is a life of waiting. Everything about following Jesus is based on a promise. Our entire existence rests on God's promises to us. We're waiting for the coming of our Savior. We're waiting to see the Lord Jesus face to face someday. We're waiting for eternity. We're waiting to be transformed into His likeness.

The Christian life is a life of waiting.

This week, we move from the Old to the New Testament as we continue to follow the footsteps of God and His faithfulness to His people through the pages of Scripture. The people of Israel have spent a lot of time in the desert and have experienced God's faithfulness despite their disobedience and stiff-neckedness. In our previous stop, the people of Israel were about to be taken into captivity and exile but had been given a promise for redemption. Jeremiah 31 was God's offer of mercy to His people in the wilderness.

Between the pages of Jeremiah 31 and the beginning of the New Testament comes a season of waiting. But by *season*, I'm not referring to a quarterly cycle of three months. For the people of Israel, their season of waiting ended up lasting four hundred years before they saw the first big step in God's fulfillment of His promise. And even then, most of them still missed the coming of the Messiah.

We'll be spending this week in Luke 3 and the ministry of John the Baptist. If you've ever endured a long period of silence from God, you're going to love this week's lesson. If you're stuck in a desert of waiting in a culture that's hurting and you're beginning to wonder if God really meant what He once promised you, then sit up. Listen up. You're about to be set free!

Day 1: Wilderness of Waiting

Reading: Luke 1:1–25

Theme: Even in seasons of silence and waiting, God is working to accomplish His purposes.

If there's anything worse than waiting, it's waiting without direction. It's waiting without any sense of when the waiting will end. It's waiting that goes on forever. That's the kind of waiting most of us are familiar with.

We left the people of Israel in Jeremiah 31 immediately before their exile to Babylon. The Babylonian captivity lasted seventy years, after which a small remnant of the people made the trek back to Jerusalem under the leadership of Ezra and, later, Nehemiah.

Though the canon of Scripture puts Ezra, Nehemiah, and Esther in the middle of the Old Testament, their events actually happened in the fourth century BC, right before the end of the Old Testament.

Then came a season of silence.

For almost 430 years, we have no recorded word from God. For almost 430 years, if we don't look at historical records outside of the Bible itself, we lose track of the happenings of the people of Israel. In Amos 8:11, we're given a glimpse of the state of affairs during that season.

Read Amos 8:11. Describe the culture that was prevalent in the years between the Old and the New Testaments.

How does this verse resonate with our present culture?

Just because we don't see a record of God's Word in that four-hundred-year season does not indicate that God was not at work in His people. When we pick up the story again in the first few pages of the New Testament, we meet some amazing men and women who have remained faithful to God. They have continued to strain to hear God's voice and to live in obedience to Him. They still believe in the faithfulness of God to His people. Let's get to know them a little bit more.

◉ Read Luke 1:1–25. Who are the characters in this story? What can you tell about their relationship with God through this passage?

◉ What problem did the couple have, and what miracle did God promise they would see?

◉ What did God promise Zechariah and Elizabeth about their son?

Zechariah responded as I would have. He hesitated to believe that God could do the impossible. Though he still believed God enough to offer yearly sacrifices to Him, when it came to the deepest desires of his heart, he doubted God. He was tempted to choose the safety of disbelief than to wager it all on the goodness of God. After years of unfulfilled longings, God's goodness seemed too good to be true.

♀ Read Luke 1:13 and 19–20. How did God respond to Zechariah's doubt?

God is patient with our doubts. When Zechariah refuses to trust God's promise, God simply invited Zechariah into a season of silence. I imagine this time of silence would free up Zechariah's time tremendously and give him the opportunity to reflect on who God is and what He had promised.

Little did Zechariah know the part he would end up playing in the bigger story of God. Jesus was about to be born. The New Covenant was about to be fulfilled. After 430 years of silence, God was about to speak to His people again, and this time through Immanuel!

♀ Read Luke 1:57–80. How did Zechariah's season of silence and waiting change him?

♀ Focus on verse 80. Why do you think John the Baptist was sent to the wilderness?

Most of us resent the wilderness. We think of it as a problem to be avoided. Despite learning how rich the desert places of life can be in terms of our relationship with God, we still long to escape our desert places. We assume the desert is God's punishment to us and a sign of His disfavor. We miss the pattern that emerges throughout Scripture: that God sends us to the desert for a reason. He prepares us for our purpose in the desert places of our lives. The desert is God's intentional place to accomplish His calling in us.

God does not hate the wilderness. Far from it, He sees it as His gift to us in a world that is noisy and distracted. He sees it as the best place for us to hear His voice calling us closer to Himself.

John was a unique young man. He grew up in the wilderness far from his peers. He was set apart by God for a specific reason. Let's learn a little bit more about John the Baptist today.

◉ Read Matthew 3:1–4. Describe your impressions of John the Baptist from this passage.

Do you wonder what Zechariah and Elizabeth thought about their introverted son who couldn't be bothered with proper culture? Do you wonder what the neighbors thought about this unusual kid who didn't care about the right outfits and appearances? Imagine growing up like John did, without the usual forms of entertainment. No team sports or school dances. No graduations or higher education. I bet it didn't feel like an honor to be set apart in the desert in the best years of a young man's life! It's hard to believe that God intended those to be good years for John. They were formative years. The desert was God's gift as He grew John into the kind of man who could radically change his culture.

◉ Read Luke 3:1–6. What do you think God said to John during those years in the desert? How did God's Word impact John the Baptist?

I've always thought of the 430 years between the Old and the New Testaments as a season of silence, but God's Word was still available and familiar to many who looked for it.

◉ Read Isaiah 40:1–8. How do you think John became familiar enough with this passage that he quoted it to the people?

◉ What does verse 8 tell you about the power and relevance of God's Word?

◉ Why do you think God set the stage for the coming of Jesus to take place out in the wilderness?

We've been focused on God's faithfulness to His people in desert places. From the call of Abraham in Genesis 12 and throughout the Old Testament, we witnessed how God uses the desert places for the good of His children. We learned that the secret to peace lies in depending on God in the desert places. We got a taste of God's goodness to His people exemplified in His daily provision of manna. We experienced God's mercy to His people in the desert of their brokenness.

The desert is God's intentional place to accomplish His calling in us.

Here, in the early pages of the New Testament, once again, we see God proving Himself to be a faithful Father who uses the desert places as His invitation into deeper communion with Him. Even more, we will become familiar with the desert as the place God chooses to lead His people to revival again.

If you've been living in a desert of unending waiting and unfulfilled desires, it's not time to give up. If you've been straining to hear God's voice after years of silence, you might be closer to breakthrough than you think. Like John the Baptist, maybe it is God's faithfulness that has led you to the desert in order to reveal Himself to you afresh. If you're hungry for more of God in your life, your desert might just be the perfect place for God to draw you back to Himself.

Let's Make This Personal

📍 Where in your life is there a famine for the Word of God? What's keeping you from feasting on the Word of God daily?

📍 When was the last time you spent extensive time alone with the Word of God? In what ways were you changed?

● Has God ever promised you something that seemed too good to be true? How has the story of John's parents encouraged you?

● How deeply do you long to know God? How does it change your perspective when you understand that the desert of silence and waiting is God's gift to draw you closer to Him?

Today's Take Home Point

Holding on to God's Word even when God is silent is the secret to your breakthrough.

Final Thought

● What is God inviting you to through your seasons of prolonged waiting and uncomfortable silence?

Day 2: Ears Wide Open

Reading: Luke 3:1–22

Theme: It is in our most desperate desert places that we're most willing to hear God's voice.

As a verbal processor, I'm always grateful that God's power is best experienced through His Word. God speaks. From the opening lines of Scripture, we encounter a God who speaks. That's pretty incredible!

"In the beginning, God created the heavens and the earth. The earth was without form and void, and darkness was over the face of the deep. And the Spirit of God was hovering over the face of the waters. And God said, 'Let there be light,' and there was light" (Gen. 1:1–3).

The expression "God said" is used ten times in the opening chapter of Genesis. The words of God bring about creation. We see the same thing in John 1:1—"In the beginning was the Word, and the Word was with God, and the Word was God."

The association of God with His Word is as surprising as it is a relief. We have a God who speaks. Not only is He alive and purposeful, but He tells us stuff! What woman doesn't love to hear that?

After four hundred years of silence, God resumed His conversation with His people through His relationship with Zechariah and Elizabeth, and then their son, John the Baptist. While we refer to the time between the Old and the New Testaments as years of silence, the truth is that God wasn't silent during those years. The words of the prophets were still available for those who wanted to hear God's voice. God also used the natural creation to speak to anyone who bothered to look for Him (Rom. 1:20). Elizabeth and Zechariah were familiar with God's Word. Mary the mother of Jesus was familiar with God's Word. Joseph the husband of Mary was familiar with God's Word.

The problem with the people of Israel is that they didn't want to hear. Until they found themselves at their wits' end, they didn't bother to look for direction. It was always in the wilderness of their lives that the people of Israel developed ears to hear what God had to say.

◉ Read Jeremiah 5:21. What does it mean to have eyes but not see and to have ears but not hear?

You would think that the only way God would get His people to listen to Him again was to lead them back into the wilderness. And that's exactly what God did in Luke 3.

◉ Read Matthew 3:1–6. How did the people of Israel respond to John's message (see v. 5)? What do you think explained their willingness to listen to John the Baptist?

While John the Baptist makes an appearance in the early pages of the New Testament, he's also the last of the Old Testament prophets. Maybe it was the hunger of God's people for God's Word that led them to run to the desert and listen. Maybe it was the darkness of their days that created a sense of despair and desperate need for a move from God. Or maybe it was simply God who was drawing His people back to Himself again because of His faithfulness to them. Whatever the reason, it was about time!

◉ Read Luke 3:2–9. What sort of message was John the Baptist preaching to the people? Was this a popular message or a difficult one?

As an ER doctor, I have found that people listen better to their doctors when they are really sick. People who are not very ill tend to argue with their doctors about their diagnosis and treatment plans. They're picky about the instructions they receive. They're critical and high-maintenance. They express their opinions loudly even when they're wrong. I'm limited in my ability to care for people who are well enough to get by.

But give me a dying patient, and everything changes. Desperation has a way of opening our ears to the truth. When my patients are really sick, they lose their taste for argument. They're quick to lean in and listen to my words of healing. They do what I ask. They ask questions not in an effort to frustrate me but in order to gain better understanding of what they need. I have a deep sense of joy and satisfaction in caring for those who want it.

As long as they could eke by on their own, God's people made do without God. It was their need that led the people of Israel to their knees.

📍 Read Luke 3:7–9. What was John the Baptist's message to the people? Describe the tone and content. Was this an easy message to listen to?

📍 Read Luke 3:10–14. What was the response of the people to the message?

Too many of us wait until disaster hits to seek the help that we need. But you don't have to be dying to listen well—you simply have to be willing!

◉ Read Hebrews 3:15–19. What's the connection between our ears and our hearts?

◉ How quick should your response be to God's revealed truth?

The best way to recognize if you're listening to God's voice is by whether you're willing to do what He says. Faith is best revealed in your obedience to God's Word. The minute you take God at His Word, you find rest. For centuries, the people of Israel sought rest but didn't find it. The reason was that they didn't take God at His word. They had ears, but they didn't hear what God was telling them. It took the desert to get them to listen.

What if God's gift to you is the very desert place you find yourself in? What if your desert is God's invitation to stir your heart to listen? Listening ears rely on a soft heart, and nothing will soften your heart like time in the desert. If you find yourself in the wilderness of God's silence or the wilderness of waiting or the wilderness of disobedience or the wilderness of brokenness, God's gift to you is that He will use your desert places to prepare your heart to listen to His voice again—just as He did for the people of Israel. Your future peace rests on your willingness to listen to God's voice again.

◉ God is not indifferent to the listening skills of His people. He is eager for us to hear Him. Read Isaiah 48:18. What does God promise to those who listen to His Word?

Let's finish today's time by listening. Close your eyes and listen to all God has shown you in today's lesson. Set your timer for five minutes. Fight the temptation to move or talk. When you finish this time, jot down what you heard God say.

Let's Make This Personal

📍 What are some of the ways God's Word has been a lifeline for you in times of need? Share a few verses that anchor you when you're in trouble.

📍 Have you ever gotten to the place in your life where you're desperate enough to listen to God's voice? What has led you to this place?

📍 Think about your response to God's Word in your life. Are you in a place of tenderhearted submission? How can you tell?

📍 How would you rate your listening in this season of your life? What is keeping you from listening well?

📍 How obedient are you to what God is saying in this season of your life?

Today's Take Home Point

Your obedience to God best reflects
how well you have heard Him.

Final Thought

📍 As you lean in to hear Him more clearly, what new practice or habit is God inviting you to?

Day 3: Wide Awake

Reading: Matthew 3:1–17

Theme: It takes the barrenness of the desert to truly awaken us to our need for a Savior.

Do you ever have days when you get out of bed, get dressed, have your coffee, drive to work, and still you're not quite awake? It happens to me some days. On those days, it feels like I'm sleepwalking through my life. During those days—or seasons—I go through all the right motions. I've been trained over the years to say the right things and do the right things. But it's as if my senses are dulled.

Some Christians live their whole lives that way. They know when to show up and when to raise their hands during worship. They can lead prayer meetings and teach Bible studies. They might even make it all the way to heaven just going through the right motions. Like patients in a coma, they're alive but not fully awake. I don't want that to happen to me.

It will sometimes take a crisis to awaken us to the things that matter in life, or sometimes it simply takes the desert.

Read Matthew 3:1–3. What was the message that John the Baptist preached? What did he mean by *the kingdom of heaven*?

Read Matthew 3:6. How did the people respond to the ministry of John the Baptist? What do you think was the reason for that response?

📍 Read Luke 3:15. Whom were the people waiting in expectation for and why?

Think about it. For over four hundred years, the people of Israel had no word from the Lord. There were no fresh recorded words by prophets. For over four hundred years, the people of Israel had no obvious spiritual awakening. They had no new revelation from God. The promise God had made to Abraham centuries before might have sounded like wishful thinking or a tale one shares with their grandkids of what might have been.

As far as we can tell, the people of Israel were spiritually dormant for four hundred years. Certainly, God did not speak any new Scripture during that time. The people needed an awakening. God's gift to the people of Israel was an invitation to the desert, where they would hear the words of a scruffy prophet with boldness not seen since the days of Elijah. John wore funny clothes and ate unusual food, but one thing was for sure: his message in the desert was bringing life to people who desperately needed it.

📍 Read Luke 3:1–2. Who was ruling and what was the political climate during the time of John the Baptist's ministry?

The fifteenth year of the reign of Tiberias places the time around AD 27–29. Tiberius was an emperor known for his cruelty. Pontius Pilate, later made famous by the crucifixion, was known for his brutal massacres of the Jewish people in Judea.

Herod, Philip, and Archelaus were descendants of Herod the Great, known for their corruption and cruelty. After Herod the Great died, he divided the kingdom among his three sons, Herod Antipas, Archelaus, and Philip. Herod Antipas is the guy who later killed John the Baptist.

Caiaphas and Annas were the religious leaders of the day, both of whom appear later in the ministry of Jesus. They were both corrupt, more interested in politics than in serving God.[10] They were also under Roman occupation. All this is to say that the Jewish people lived under extremely difficult times. They were stuck in not only a spiritual desert but a political and cultural one, as well.

What is it about the desert that makes it an ideal place to come alive?

What keeps us from awakening to God when life is good and circumstances are easy?

Read Romans 13:11. Why is there such a sense of urgency for us to come alive? What accounts for our lack of urgency in spiritual matters on any given day?

Most of us believe that Jesus will indeed come back someday, but not for another one hundred years at least. Even though my mother tells me we're living in the End Times, I'm far too practical to live with a sense of an impending eternity. It hardly occurs to me that the divine things in life are happening all around me. It's only when I find myself in the middle of a crisis, in the desert of need, that I am finally ready to wake up.

The Jewish people were plagued with the same lack of awareness. Think about it. Even though they lived in the days of John the Baptist, witnessed his crusade, and were even moved to change by his message, little did they know even then that the Messiah was already living in their midst. Their sense of understanding was stunted.

It took the desert to awaken their expectations. It took the desert to help them come alive!

Read Luke 3:7. How did the people who received the message of John the Baptist express their newfound faith?

Let's talk about baptism for a moment. Where did it come from? John the Baptist is the first person in the New Testament to administer and talk about baptism. The concept of baptism wasn't new for the people of Israel, though. Even before John's ministry, the Jewish people used baptism as an act of purification and initiation of converts to Judaism.[11] In other words, if a non-Jew converted to Judaism, baptism was the radical act of individual commitment he or she made to belong to the people of God.

When John extended the invitation to his own people to be baptized, he was waking them up to their need for salvation. He was letting them know just how far they had drifted from God. He was pleading with them to change.[12] This was a radical step for a Jewish person to take. It was a sign of understanding that all the religion in the world had not changed their hearts. It was an acknowledgment that the status quo was no longer okay. It was an affront to the religious leaders in that day. But things were just getting started!

To paraphrase the prophet Isaiah, John's ministry was a highway in the desert proclaiming the end of spiritual exile and a preparation for the kingdom of God. Baptism symbolized change and a return to God.

◉ Read Acts 2:38. What do you learn about baptism here? Does baptism save the follower of Jesus?

Slowly but surely, the people who had come out to the wilderness were coming alive. Their hearts were drawn by God, and their eyes opened to spiritual realities. God was using the barrenness of the desert to awaken His people to Himself.

God is still awakening His people through the desert. It's in the desert where we can finally turn down the distracting voices of our culture. It's in the desert where we have time to listen to His voice. It's in the desert where our desperation becomes palpable enough to move us to change.

◉ Read Luke 3:18. What made the good news John preached so good?

◉ Read Luke 3:19–20. Not everyone responded with repentance. Who was mad about John, and what did he do to John?

John's imprisonment happens just as Jesus' ministry takes off. I guess you could say that John the Baptist was about to enter into his own desert for a season. I used to think this was unfair. I hurt for this bold man of God who had given his life for Jesus. But the more I know about God's invitation to the desert and His purposes for it, I wonder if perhaps I'm beginning to think differently about it.

The gift of the desert was the gift of an awakened heart for the Jewish people. In Ephesians 5:14, Paul wrote: "Awake, O sleeper, and arise from the dead, and Christ will shine on you."

In more ways than one, that's exactly what happened to the Jewish people. It was in the desert that their ears were opened and their hearts awakened. Even more importantly, Christ was about to literally shine on them!

The best was yet to come.

Let's Make This Personal

◉ What are some of the distractions of life that keep you from waking up to God?

◉ What does being spiritually awake look like for you?

◉ On a scale of 1–10 (1 = fast asleep, 10 = wide awake), how awake would you rate yourself spiritually?

◉ How would you live differently if your spiritual eyes were opened to spiritual realities afresh? What habits would you change? What practices would you adopt?

◉ Have you ever felt opposition for sharing the good news of the gospel? How did you respond to the pressure you faced?

Today's Take Home Point

The desert is the place where distractions die down enough for us to pay attention to spiritual realities.

Final Thought

◉ What is God's invitation to you in reordering your priorities?

Day 4: Total Change

Reading: Luke 3:3–14

Theme: The gift of the desert is the gift of brokenness that leads us to change.

A friend of mine stopped by my house recently and unloaded his struggles. After pouring out his woes, he concluded with great conviction: "People never change. No matter how much we try to convince ourselves they will, they simply don't."

My friend either does not fully understand salvation or he's been too wounded to believe that change is possible. Cynicism is born out of hurt. It's a self-protective mechanism we use to guard against future failure. It's easier to state that it's not possible to change than to admit that, so far, it's been really hard for me to change.

Yet change is at the heart of what it means to be a follower of Jesus Christ.

Read 2 Corinthians 5:17. What does Paul say about the Christian life and change?

Read Romans 12:1–2. In what ways does God invite us to change? How is that change possible?

What has been the hardest area for you to change in?

That we're invited by God to change does not make the process of change any easier. Over the years I've encountered many reasons change is challenging:

- I'm not really serious about change.
- I've tried to change and failed.
- I'm not sure how to change.
- I'm tired of trying so hard without obvious results.
- I feel like a hypocrite talking about change while still being unable to execute it.

📍 What obstacles stand between you and the change you desire?

We've been spending the week in Luke 3. The point of Bible study is not just to learn the facts of the Bible but to allow God's Spirit to change us through His Word. We want our hearts changed by God. We're looking for a fresh encounter with God. We long for revival. The Bible, after all, isn't a rule book but a love letter. It's the story of God's heart for us, His people, and His desire for us to change.

Even in the short time we've been together so far, we've tracked God's steps dealing with His people through desert places and have seen change all over the place.

- Abraham changed his address.
- Abraham changed his direction and places of worship.
- The people of Israel changed their nationality.
- The people of Israel changed in their lifestyles.
- The Old Covenant was replaced by the New Covenant.

God's desire is for us to be free from the burdens of a life without His presence and to be rich with the joy of His presence. He longs for us to be free from oppression and the shackles of sin and invites us into a life of hope. He seeks to break the cycles of disappointment and despair in our desert places by teaching us not to expect Him to do things He never promised in the first place. He then replaces our disappointment with a sense of fulfillment and abiding peace.

But how? How does God call us to change? Well, it happens in the desert. Change is most pronounced when the awareness of our need to change is greatest. Change happens out of brokenness, and nothing positions us to reach a place of brokenness as well as the desert places.

📍 Read Luke 3:3–14. How would you define repentance based on this reading?

We're living in a time of political correctness. No one wants to offend anyone. We've gotten really good at softening the message of the gospel into a seeker-sensitive, politically correct, grace-filled presentation. Don't get me wrong. I'm all about grace. But sometimes the truth won't change you until it hurts you.

📍 How politically correct was John the Baptist's message in Luke 3? Why did John call his listeners a "brood of vipers"?

Ironically, the people who had shown up to the desert weren't offended by John—they were convicted. Their response was radical. They longed to know the secret to this salvation. They wanted more. Instead of rejecting John and his message, they took a public step of faith by getting baptized.

♥ What did John say that caused the hearts of the people to change?

♥ Read Romans 2:4. What is it that leads us to repent?

If I were to jot down the progression of what happened to the people listening to John, I might plot it out like this:

- They were invited to the wilderness.
- They heard the gospel message preached.
- Their ears were opened to listen.
- Their hearts were awakened to receive.
- Their wills were broken in agreement.
- Their lives were changed.

Brokenness led them to change.

I love the concept of brokenness. It's the opposite of being hard-hearted. It's impossible to reach a place of brokenness without humility. It's impossible to become broken without the willingness to bend the knee in submission.

Sometimes the truth won't change you until it hurts you.

As the people heard and understood John's message, their spiritual eyes were opened. They saw themselves as sinners in need of a Savior. It was their willingness to humble their hearts and humbly agree with God's Word that led them to freedom.

It's impossible to repent without submitting to God's ways. Our obedient actions flow out of our belief that God's Word is true. Repentance is the willingness to pay whatever price it costs to make things right again.

Until we get to the point where our desire to change becomes greater than our desire to be right, we won't change. Until we get to the point where we're willing to pay any price to experience a deeper relationship with God, we're not truly repentant.

○ Read Luke 3:10–14. In what areas of their lives did the people need to repent?

I wish I could tell you that I had a magic bullet for change. I wish there was a way to make the process easy. There isn't. There is no magic bullet. Only a lifestyle of repentance and humble daily submission to God will transform us into Christlikeness.

○ Read 2 Corinthians 3:16–4:1. What does turning to God look like practically, and what is the outcome of turning our attention on the Lord?

Life didn't become easy for the people who got baptized by John. Their problems didn't disappear. Their need for more change didn't end on that day. It would be awhile before they fully understood all that God still had in store for them. It would take Jesus and His death and resurrection to help them come alive.

But on that day in the middle of the desert, the people who heard the Word of God and submitted to Him were given a gift—the gift of repentance and change.

Are you ready to receive that gift too? Are you willing to repent?

Let's Make This Personal

📍 Describe a season of brokenness in your life.

📍 In what areas of your life do you currently see brokenness?

📍 How have your desert places been an invitation for you to change?

📍 As you consider where the Spirit of God is asking you to repent, are you willing to do it, or does it feel like God is asking too much of you?

Today's Take Home Point

Brokenness is God's invitation for us to change.

Final Thought

What is God's invitation to you in the places you need to change?

Day 5: World-Changers

Reading: Luke 7:18–35

Theme: The desert is the perfect backdrop to change the world.

God is always working in a million different ways while we're focused on our one thing. I tend to make my life about my needs. My prayers are focused on God providing my daily bread. It's not that I don't care about others; it's just that I'm focused on my little patch of the desert, and on most days, the heat in my own desert is high enough to melt my attention for others.

God, on the other hand, keeps track of it all. He sees the entire scope of humanity and knows exactly where you and I fit. He is concerned about *all* our needs. He is aware of every little detail in our lives. He has the power to provide for my personal needs without tipping the global scale. He has enough for everyone's needs. His way is the way of abundance!

We've spent this week in Luke 3 and Matthew 3. We've been paying attention to John the Baptist while continuing to track God's dealings with His people after four hundred years of silence. We met John's family earlier this week. It's interesting to note that John the Baptist not only lived in the desert—he was also birthed out of a desert place. His mother was in a desert of literal barrenness when God turned her pain into joy.

Pain often brings us to our knees, doesn't it? It's what fuels us to draw closer to God. It's what propels us to seek healing. So much good can be born out of pain. A few years ago, *The Prayer of Jabez* became really popular (who doesn't love the promise that if you claim it, you might actually receive it?). If you're not familiar with it, you might enjoy reading it.

◉ Read 1 Chronicles 4:9–10. What was it that led Jabez's mother to pray?

◉ Can you think of anything good that has been born out of *your* painful places?

I hope you're beginning to understand by now the richness of the gift of desert places. God invites us to the desert places not only for a purpose but also as a gift—a gift that is meant to awaken us to life. The desert leads us into a closer walk with God. The desert is where we see Jesus more clearly.

For John the Baptist, the desert was indeed the place where his eyes first recognized the Messiah. The story of John recognizing Jesus as the Messiah is so critical that it's told in all four Gospels, perhaps as a proclamation of the coming of the King.

◉ Read Matthew 3:11–17; Mark 1:7–11; Luke 3:15–22; and John 1:19–34. What is similar between the passages from all four Gospels? What details are unique in some of the Gospels?

◉ Because John the Baptist's mother, Elizabeth, was related to Mary, Jesus and John the Baptist were actually cousins. What might have gone through John's mind when he finally recognized that his cousin Jesus was the Messiah?

◉ What do you learn about John's heart from his understanding of his role in God's kingdom?

I'm amazed with the life of John the Baptist. In a culture rife with influencers and platforms, John the Baptist seemed to do everything upside down. Instead of preaching in a cosmopolitan city, John's home base was the desert. Instead of using seeker-sensitive language, John called his listeners a brood of vipers. Instead of sending them home to process the message they had heard, John baptized them on the spot! Instead of cozying up to Jesus for a prime role in Jesus' earthly ministry, John simply fades into the background once Jesus comes onto the scene.

◉ Read John 3:22–36. What was it about John that allowed him to see things differently than how the culture did?

◉ Read John 3:30. This is one of the most powerful statements in the New Testament. What does it reveal about John's identity?

John the Baptist was a world-changer.

Being a world-changer is never easy. John's life in the wilderness was a lonely one. He dressed funny and ate a weird diet. But what made him so radically different from the world he lived in was not his wardrobe, menu, or address. It was his heart. He saw things more clearly than everyone around him did. He heard God's voice more clearly than everyone else did. He obeyed Him more readily than everyone else did. Perhaps it was the gift of the wilderness that taught John who he really was.

♀ After spending time this week meditating on the life of John, what are some of the ways you see that he changed the world?

♀ What did it cost John the Baptist to live a life that stood so contrary to his culture?

The life of obedience to Christ isn't always easy, and it doesn't always end well—humanly speaking. For John, things got really bad, really fast. The next segment of John's life is one of the hardest stories in Scripture to hear. It's also one of the most encouraging stories when you find yourself in the desert.

♀ Read Luke 3:18–20 and Luke 7:18–35. What happened to John?

📍 What was going through John's mind while he was in prison? Do you blame him for having doubts?

📍 How did Jesus respond to John's disciples?

📍 How do you think John may have reacted to the message Jesus sent?

The words of Jesus aren't always easy to hear, are they? Sometimes, our calling is hard. The Christian life can feel lonely and unfair. It's only in the light of eternity that our lives make total sense. It's only in the shadow of the cross that we see the resurrection.

John the Baptist never left that prison. In fact, it wasn't much later that he was beheaded by Herod. You can read the events in Matthew 14:1–12. It's a sad story.

📍 Read Matthew 14:13. How did Jesus respond to the news of John's death?

◉ I love Jesus so much. Even when we don't understand His ways, we're assured of His love. His reaction to John's death fills me with peace. What emotions fill your heart when you think about Jesus alone with His Father, mourning the death of John?

◉ The message of Christianity is not easy. It's good, but it's hard. Jesus Himself warned us of the cost of following Him. Read Matthew 16:24–26. Summarize the message Jesus gave us.

◉ How closely did John the Baptist live the words of Matthew 16:24–26?

John the Baptist's life may have seemed like a waste to a nonbelieving world, but in the eyes of our Savior Jesus, he was the greatest man who ever lived. Read Luke 7:26–28.

The desert leads us into a closer walk with God. The desert is where we see Jesus more clearly.

If you've ever felt disappointed in your Christian life, I hope the story of John the Baptist has touched your heart deeply. If you're stuck in the desert when you thought God had big plans for you, I hope you're beginning to see what a gift the desert is to you.

I also hope you're beginning to understand that God's dreams for your life are bigger than *your* dreams for your life. His vision for you is eternal. His plans for you extend past what you deem so vital here on this earth. His ways are upside down. It's in losing your life that you'll find it. It's when you're at your weakest that you'll experience His strength. Your time in the desert is never wasted. An entire culture is watching to see how you'll respond to your desert season.

God might still use you to change the world, even in your desert places.

Let's Make This Personal

📍 How has the life of John the Baptist encouraged you?

📍 Which are you living: a life that is trying to gain the world or a life that is living for eternity?

📍 Where does God want you to deny yourself and take up your cross?

⦿ Who is God inviting to your desert places to hear the good news of the gospel through your life?

⦿ What if, like John, your life never gets its happy ending here on this side? Would you be okay with that? If not, what does that mean?

Today's Take Home Point

It's not easy to change the world,
but Jesus is so very worth it!

Final Thought

⦿ What is God's invitation to you as you count the cost of following Jesus?

Praying through Scripture—Week 4
Called to the Desert
Matthew 3:1–12

In those days John the Baptist came preaching in the wilderness of Judea, "Repent, for the kingdom of heaven is at hand." For this is he who was spoken of by the prophet Isaiah when he said,

"The voice of one crying in the wilderness:
'Prepare the way of the Lord;
    make his paths straight.'"

Now John wore a garment of camel's hair and a leather belt around his waist, and his food was locusts and wild honey. Then Jerusalem and all Judea and all the region about the Jordan were going out to him, and they were baptized by him in the river Jordan, confessing their sins.

But when he saw many of the Pharisees and Sadducees coming to his baptism, he said to them, "You brood of vipers! Who warned you to flee from the wrath to come? Bear fruit in keeping with repentance. And do not presume to say to yourselves, 'We have Abraham as our father,' for I tell you, God is able from these stones to raise up children for Abraham. Even now the axe is laid to the root of the trees. Every tree therefore that does not bear good fruit is cut down and thrown into the fire.

"I baptize you with water for repentance, but he who is coming after me is mightier than I, whose sandals I am not worthy to carry. He will baptize you with the Holy Spirit and fire. His winnowing fork is in his hand, and he will clear his threshing floor and gather his wheat into the barn, but the chaff he will burn with unquenchable fire."

Read the passage out loud once.

Now close your eyes and take a few deep breaths. Pray with me: "O God, I pray that You will help me to hear You speak during this time of meditation on Your Word. I open my hands to You. I open my ears to You."

Pause for eight to ten seconds.

Imagine you're in the crowd, listening to John's message. Earlier that week, you'd had no intention of coming out to a desert to listen to an angry preacher. You were too busy for religious activities. Between meeting the needs of your own household as well as your duties as a daughter and sister and friend, you could barely focus on anything outside of the urgent. You'd heard rumors about John the Baptizer. You had laughed with your neighbors that one evening when they'd described his fashion statement. Crazy, they'd said about him. The guy had lost his mind.

You'd grown up in the hill country of Judah and remembered little John as a boy. He was always a bit funny. His parents never cut his hair. The story was that his mother had him when she was well past the age of childbearing. I suppose that explained her overprotectiveness of him.

When he started camping out in the wilderness, you assumed he was eccentric. You lost track of him for a while. But recently, everyone was talking about him again. Some had even gone out to see him. You had no intention of going anywhere near that crazy man, though. You had too much to do. Your life had no room for luxuries like visiting a crazy preacher.

That morning, though, everything changed. You woke up to the terrible news that your husband had been fired from his job and that your mother's illness had taken a turn for the worse. That morning, you got the news that Rome was imposing a new tax. You barely had enough money to pay for food for the family, let alone find the funds for this tax.

When your best friend showed up to your doorstep, you were more than ready for a distraction. When she invited you to go with her to visit the baptizer, you had nothing left to lose. A little entertainment wouldn't hurt.

Read the passage again.

Pause for eight to ten seconds.

Take a deep breath as you listen to the words of John the Baptist. Look at him carefully. What do you see? What makes his words so riveting? Can you see his heart? What's driving the intensity of this man's words? You find yourself leaning in. You hang on every word he's uttering. Everyone else around you is equally riveted. You can almost hear a pin drop. What part of the message resonates with you? What part of the message confuses you?

At one point, you notice a group of Pharisees and Sadducees walk up to the front. You can tell trouble is on the way. You assume John will quietly apologize and give the religious leaders the platform. But instead, you're shocked by what comes out of John's mouth.

Read the passage again.

Pause for eight to ten seconds.

How do you respond to John's words? Do they bring you relief and a sort of vindication? Do you feel afraid for John?

Now you look up and notice a long line of people waiting to be baptized. You're not familiar with this ritual of baptism, but something about it feels like a fresh start. Something about this act of baptism feels like a second chance.

Before you know it, you see yourself walk up to the line of people waiting to be baptized. You're not 100 percent sure of what you're doing, but you know you can't keep living as you are. You're exhausted. You're overwhelmed all the time. You could almost say you need a Savior.

When John starts talking about someone coming who is mightier than he is, you look up. Your heart almost misses a beat. Who could be greater than John the Baptizer? This man you thought was crazy turned out to be bolder than you imagined. The message he shares resonates with you at a level so deep it feels like a message from God.

Could this man he's talking about be … no, that doesn't even seem possible. For a moment, you second-guess yourself. You're losing your mind. This can't be true. Real life doesn't work that way. Real life ends in heartbreak for people like you. Real life offers no saviors.

Unless … unless the story you were told when you were a kid about the coming of a Messiah is true.

Pause for eight to ten seconds.

How does the idea of a Savior fill you with joy? Where in your life do you need a Savior? What are you willing to give up in order to gain such a Savior?

Session 5

The Gift of Desert Places

Luke 3:1–22

Watch the session 5 video now. The video is available at DavidCCook.org/access, with access code DesertPlaces.

1. It is because of the desert places that I'm better able to see my _____ for a Savior.

2. It is because of the desert places that I'm better positioned to reach a place of _____.

3. It is because of the desert places that I'm better able to prioritize what's _____.

4. It is because of the desert places that I'm better _____ to declare the faithfulness of God to a watching generation.

Video Group Discussion Questions

After watching the video, discuss the following questions in your group.

📍 When have you seen your need for Jesus most clearly?

📍 What does brokenness look like in your life right now?

📍 Think about your priorities. If someone were to look at your schedule and the way you spend your time, what would they say were your top three priorities? What are the top three priorities you'd like to see in your life?

📍 John lived an upside-down life compared to his culture. What are some of the ways your life as a Christian should clash with the culture around you?

📍 Do you think God wants you to be a world-changer, or is He okay with you being a willing servant? How does your idea of what a world-changer is differ from God's idea?

Week 5: Overcoming in Desert Places

1 Peter 4:19
"Therefore let those who suffer according to God's will entrust their souls to a faithful Creator while doing good."

Introduction

In this book, we've been making our way to Jesus. We started in Genesis, where God promised redemption to Adam and Eve through the coming of Jesus the Messiah. In Genesis 12, God promised Abraham a son, and although Isaac was special, it was the promise of the coming Jesus through Abraham's seed that was the greater miracle.

In Exodus, Abraham's little family had grown into a nation. Under the leadership of Moses, the people of Israel marched straight out of the bondage of Egypt toward the Promised Land and through the wilderness. Their time in the desert served a purpose. It made them stronger. Alas, forty days turned to forty years in the desert and became a cycle of failure and victory.

By the time Jeremiah started his ministry, the people of Israel were on a downward slope, spiritually and politically. Right before they were taken into exile, they were offered words of hope in Jeremiah 31. Jeremiah's message was a canvas of God's mercy at a time when it was desperately needed. It was also a reminder of God's promise to His people of the coming Messiah and ultimate redemption.

It took another 430 years for God's promise to be fulfilled. But after years of silence, God did speak. John the Baptist would declare the message of salvation right from the wilderness and proclaim the coming of the King. This man had fire in his bones. Like the prophets before him, he stood strong in the face of a hurting culture and reminded his people of their God. John was used by God to turn the light on for God's people, who had become accustomed to the darkness.

A shift was taking place. A movement was swelling. Though the people were turning to God, they didn't realize that God was already in their midst. A young man named Jesus had been born to a virgin named Mary thirty years earlier. And He was about to save the world.

God's ways have never been like our ways. His thoughts are not our thoughts. His timing is not like ours. Where we keep looking for answers, God has already provided the answer. Where we see the desert, God sees salvation.

The greatest mystery of God remains that He reveals Himself to His people. The greatest miracle of God is that He has revealed Himself to us. Even before we become aware enough of His presence to worship Him, He lovingly shows us over and over again that He is a God who always keeps His promises. He is faithful.

And His faithfulness is seen in every step of the wilderness. He is present right here in your desert places—inviting you to deeper communion with Him, working out His will through your desert, and using the very desert you hate to change you and the world around you.

Where we see the desert, God sees salvation.

We reach a climax in our study this week. We're going to focus on Jesus in His wilderness. We're about to learn how to overcome in desert places.

Day 1: Every Christian's Battlefield

Reading: Matthew 4:1–17

Theme: God's plan for us in the desert of temptation is victory.

I love the desert. I mean I *literally* love the desert. Every few months, I book a flight to Phoenix because I hear the desert calling to me. It doesn't matter whether it's 80 degrees or 108, you'll find me hiking the arid trails with a smile on my face. I love everything about the cacti, the canyons, and the sound of barrenness. My mom, on the other hand, doesn't care for the desert. She thinks it's too hot and too brown. She'd rather spend her days at the beach.

Whether you agree with me or prefer my mom's idea of a vacation, if you're a follower of Jesus Christ, you'd better get used to the desert—because God has an affinity for desert places too. I know this because we've been following the footsteps of God in desert places through His Word. In our time together, we've seen the riches of God in life's desert places. We've deepened our understanding of God's faithfulness to His children in the desert. We've learned to be thankful for our desert places and to know that the desert places of our lives are where we will receive a deeper revelation of who God is.

God takes things a step further, though. This week, we're going to see why God leads His most beloved into the desert. We're going to become familiar with the deserts of temptation. More importantly, we're going to learn how to become victorious in our deserts of temptation.

📍 Read Matthew 3:16–4:11. Describe the relationship between Jesus and His Father right before Jesus goes into the wilderness.

📍 What has Jesus accomplished in His life at the time that the Father says: "This is my beloved Son, with whom I am well pleased" (Matt. 3:17)?

📍 What does God's statement of pleasure in His Son tell us about God's love for us?

📍 Focus on Matthew 4:1. Who was it who led Jesus into the desert?

📍 It seems hard to believe that right after God declares His pleasure in His Son, the Spirit sends Jesus into a face-off with Satan. Why do you think it was God's plan to send Jesus to the wilderness to be tempted by the devil? (Read Hebrews 2:14–18 for more perspective.)

Don't you hate temptation? I do. As a follower of Jesus, I have faced temptation as far back as I can remember. I am quite accustomed to the desert of temptation. I also know how much I hate it. I bet you do too. Yet if God sent Jesus into the desert of temptation, there has to be a really good reason for it.

📍 Read Hebrews 5:8. Why do you think God allowed Jesus to suffer in the wilderness of temptation?

Q Read Matthew 4:1. Though Jesus was led by God into the wilderness, who was the source of the temptation?

Q Read James 1:13–15. According to James, the brother of Jesus, what else is the source of temptation?

Q While God allows us to be tempted, He never leads us to sin. In fact, God's Word tells us the opposite. Read 1 Corinthians 10:13. What does God promise us in regard to temptation?

While God might send us to the wilderness to face the evil one, He's not the author of temptation. Our desires are evil. Satan's attack is powerful. Yet God used the wilderness in the life of Jesus to show us how to become victorious when we're facing temptation. But He did even more for us in the desert. He Himself became victorious over temptation in order to ensure that we may live victoriously over the tempter too.

Q Read Hebrews 4:14–16. What do you learn about Jesus in these verses?

Do you like numbers? Here is a fun tidbit: After God's people left Egypt, His plan was to take them through the wilderness for a forty-day journey. Alas, the people of Israel failed God in the wilderness, and forty days became forty years. It's not an accident that God allowed Jesus, too, to remain forty days in the wilderness. In those forty days, Jesus did what His people could not accomplish on their own. He overcame the desert and became our merciful and faithful high priest! Isn't that awesome?

Do you ever wonder why God would allow His beloved Son to suffer in the wilderness? Or maybe it's you you're worried about. Why does God allow you to continue to suffer in the desert of trial and temptation?

♦ Read Hebrews 5:8 again. What do you think it means that Jesus learned obedience through suffering?

♦ Read James 1:12. What is the reward for those who remain steadfast under temptation?

In the coming week, we will learn how Jesus defeated Satan in the wilderness. His victory will become ours. His power will become our strength to overcome temptation too. No matter how heavy the weight of temptation is in your life right now, and no matter how weak you feel against those temptations, God has already made a way for you to live victoriously.

It's God's plan for us to graduate from defeat into victory. That's why He sent His beloved Son, Jesus, into the wilderness to be tempted by the evil one.

Let's Make This Personal

♦ What emotions fill your heart when you consider that God allowed His beloved Son, in whom He was pleased, to enter a season of temptation?

⦿ Where in your life are you facing the biggest temptations right now?

⦿ What is your track record against that temptation? Have you ever felt the joy of victory, or do you feel resigned to live in defeat?

Today's Take Home Point

Not only does Jesus understand your struggle with temptation, He's also given you a way to live victoriously over temptation.

Final Thought

⦿ What's God's invitation to you in the areas you're struggling with?

Day 2: Hunger Pains

Reading: Matthew 4:1–11

Theme: Satan's strategy is to attack you when you're down, and his goal is to destroy you.

Remember what I told you in our first week together? I said that the story of the Bible is the story of God and His faithfulness to His people. It is a continuous story with one main plot: God's redemption of a broken world through His Son, Jesus Christ. He longs for us, His people, to be in close communion with Him. He longs for all humanity to be reconciled to Him.

Things fell apart for Adam and Eve in the garden of Eden. Though they were born into a beautiful garden, they failed to overcome temptation. Pastor Watchman Nee compares what happened in the garden of Eden with what unfolds before our eyes in Matthew 4 in the temptation of Jesus:

> The enemy came to the garden to attack Adam, but Jesus went to the wilderness to attack the enemy. When He was led by the Spirit to the wilderness, He was full of God.... He was ready and equipped to deal with the enemy. He went into the wilderness as a warrior and, in the highest standard of morality, He defeated Satan.[13]

Between the fall of Adam in Genesis 3 and the coming of Jesus in the New Testament were many long years of waiting. The entire story of the Old Testament reveals the extent to which God would go to draw His people back to Himself. Again and again, God gave His people mercy and bailed them out of trouble. He gave words to the prophets to urge His people to repent. God allowed the enemy to pressure His people enough to cry out to Him for help. Still … the people couldn't live up to the standard of the Old Testament law. Again and again, they failed to obey God and His ways.

When Jesus came, everything changed. In Jesus, all the demands of God were met, and all the promises of God were fulfilled. In Jesus, the law was fulfilled, and new life came. The Incarnation is one of the greatest mysteries in the world. Jesus was both fully God and fully man. It was in His humanity that He bore the burden of our sin on the cross. It was in His humanity that He faced Satan in the wilderness and defeated him.

We have much to learn from the encounter between Jesus and the devil in the desert. Understanding what happened will deepen our vision of God's love for us and teach us how to live victoriously in our own deserts of temptation.

⚲ Read Matthew 4:1–11. What were the three temptations Satan used to attack Jesus?

⚲ Read 1 John 2:15–16. What three categories are listed as the "things in the world"? How does this compare with the areas of temptation in Matthew 4?

⚲ While each of us struggles with our own areas of temptation, you can boil down most of our struggles to three areas: the lust of the flesh, the lust of the eyes, and the pride of life. Write down some of the common ways in our present-day culture that those three areas of temptation might be present.

⚲ Keep in mind that Satan never plays fair. He's not out for our best. He's not on our side. He hates anything to do with Jesus. He hates God and all of God's people. Read John 10:9–11. How does Jesus describe Satan (the "thief") and his goals?

⚲ Read John 8:44. What else can you find out about the things that come out of the mouth of the evil one?

⚲ Let's go back to Matthew 4:1–11. With what you've learned about Satan in mind, does it surprise you that Satan attacked Jesus after forty days of fasting?

Jesus had not eaten in forty days when He was tempted to turn a stone into bread. It doesn't seem fair to attack a man when he's down, but that's exactly Satan's strategy. He does not play fair. His goal is to destroy us.

Ultimately, Satan's goal was to thwart God's purposes for Jesus. His goal is the same for you—he wants to thwart God's purposes in your life. He wants to make sure you feel disqualified as a Christian. He wants you to give up on pursuing God's purposes and plans for your life. And he won't play fair with you, either.

Have you ever been tempted to give up on serving God because of your track record in your battle over temptation? That's my point. Satan's job is done when you crawl back to your corner in disappointment because of yet another failure.

Few things lead me to doubt God's faithfulness to me faster than my own pattern of repetitive failure against temptation. While I often blame myself for failure to live victoriously over temptation, it's equally easy to doubt God's ability to help me overcome the evil one. Why do I struggle with sin after years of battling temptation? Why doesn't God just step in and do something in the desert of my temptations?

Read Genesis 3:1–7. Unlike Jesus, Adam and Eve were not hungry when Satan tempted them. Instead of being in the desert, they were in the garden. They lived in perfection. And still they failed miserably! What's the difference between how Adam and Eve responded to the snake in the garden and how Jesus responded to Satan in the desert?

Hunger has a way of revealing the truth about who we are. Hunger has a way of exposing our hearts. What does Jesus' response to Satan reveal about what was in His heart?

We blame a lot of things on being *hangry*—or at least I do! It must be fairly common, or we wouldn't have invented a word for the condition. We blame our irritability on hunger. We attribute hiding out to our hunger. We excuse our escapism by pointing to our hunger. We excuse our loss of self-control because of our hunger.

Jesus shows us a better way.

In Jesus, all the demands of God were met, and all the promises of God were fulfilled.

After forty days of not eating or drinking, in the middle of a dry and lonely desert, Jesus had every excuse to lose focus. The power of our Savior is that, despite the worst desert conditions, He still stood victorious against Satan's lies.

Jesus offers us hope that there is a way out. His victory over Satan was not meant to be just an example for us to emulate, but a life to embrace. Whether or not you're living in the desert of temptation right now, we have a Savior who has walked in our shoes and has promised to give us the help we need to overcome the evil one.

Let's Make This Personal

⦿ Name the top one or two areas in your life where you most commonly face temptation.

⦿ In what areas of your life do you feel "hangry"? What comes out of your heart when you're hangry?

⦿ How does the encounter between Jesus and Satan in the desert encourage you?

Today's Take Home Point

What comes out of our mouths when we're hungry reveals where our heart is.

Final Thought

⦿ What's God's invitation to you in your hunger?

Day 3: The Word Is Alive

Reading: Read Matthew 4:1–11

Theme: God's Word is the weapon we need for victory in the desert.

I used to think that if I could just get through a certain season in my life, things would finally settle down. For years, I lived with the expectation that if I could just learn all the lessons God wanted me to learn, I'd no longer suffer anymore. I treated my Christian walk like a new video game—if I could just get through the next level, I might finally graduate into an easier stage. Ha!

I've learned by now that what has needed to change is my thinking. The promise of an easy Christian life is not biblical. But the promise of victory is.

Read Matthew 4:1–11 again. Don't skip the reading because you've read it before. Instead, ask the Lord for fresh insight into His Word as you read this passage again.

⚲ Who does Satan quote in his attack against Jesus?

Have you ever gotten in a conflict with someone who used God's Word out of context to attack you? The first time it happened to me, it confused me. Had I truly been guilty of what I was being accused of? Had I disobeyed God in that fashion? While it's wise to consider these questions, what we most desperately need is wisdom. God's Word can easily be twisted. It can be manipulated to meet our needs in the moment. Just listen to politicians during an election year.

Some people use God's Word to guilt others into doing what they want. Some have used it to hurt others. One of the effects of maturing in Christ is to learn to rightly divide God's Word.

⚲ Read 2 Timothy 2:15. What does it mean to rightly divide, or "handle," God's Word?

Jesus didn't fall for Satan's lies. He knew His Father's Word so well that instead of getting defensive and upset, He simply replaced Satan's lies with the truth of God's Word.

♀ How do you think Jesus knew the Old Testament so well?

When I first started teaching the Bible, I didn't know God's Word well enough to quote it. I wasn't sure that I knew where to find the verses I would need to teach well. I called my mother and unloaded my fears. She listened quietly until I uttered these words: "I'm going to quit teaching the Sunday school class. How can I teach the Bible when I don't know it all?"

Even after all these years, her response continues to give me the confidence I need to fulfill my calling to teach God's Word: "Look up Isaiah 28:13," she said. "God will teach you what you don't know."

♀ Read Isaiah 28:13. How does this verse encourage you not to give up in the process of understanding and learning God's Word?

God, in His faithfulness, always provides all that we need. The more time we spend in God's Word, the more we grow in the knowledge of God. The more we know God, the more we trust Him to faithfully provide what we need. Whenever we apply God's Word in our battle against the evil one, we're standing in the truth of who God is.

📍 Read Hebrews 4:12. What do you think it means that the Word of God is living and powerful?

📍 When was the last time you experienced God's conviction through His Word?

A recent article in *Christianity Today* stated that between 2019 and 2020, the percentage of US adults who said they use the Bible daily dropped from 14 percent to 9 percent (State of the Bible 2020 report by Barna).[14] That's not so great. Christians aren't much better. A third of Americans who attend a Protestant church regularly (32 percent) read the Bible personally every day. A little more than 27 percent say they read it a few times a week.[15]

No wonder so many of us struggle in the desert of temptation.

It was by rightly using God's Word that Jesus defeated the evil one. It was because He knew His Father's Word that Jesus was able to confidently recognize and overthrow the lies of the enemy. Most of us are not living in a time or culture of illiteracy or persecution. Most of us own more than one Bible. Yet most of us never spend more than a few minutes each day in God's Word. No wonder we're failing when it comes to the temptations in our lives.

Whenever we apply God's Word in our battle against the evil one, we're standing in the truth of who God is.

Reading God's Word regularly is a discipline. I was twenty when I started spending time in God's Word daily. I was about to start medical school when a friend told me that exercising daily would be life-giving for me in medical school. I didn't even own running shoes at the time, but I believed her. I was also a follower of Jesus and figured that if I needed to be physically fit to make it through the four grueling years of med school, then it wouldn't hurt to be spiritually fit as well.

That summer I heard a preacher say that it took twenty-one days to create a habit. So I bought some running shoes and a new journal, and started to count down. Twenty-one days and twenty-five years later, I'm still exercising and reading my Bible daily.

My story is not that special. It was God who gave me the strength to pull it off. I simply believed God enough to change. Do you?

In order to allow God's Word to help you overcome temptation, there are two things you need: you have to know God's Word, and you have to rightly apply it. What Jesus did in the wilderness wasn't complicated. Satan fed Him a lie—Jesus identified the lie and replaced it with God's truth.

God's Word is power. It truly is. Will you allow it to accomplish its purpose in your heart and mind as you go through the desert?

Let's Make This Personal

📍 How would you describe your time in God's Word and your familiarity with it?

📍 What are the main reasons you don't spend more time in God's Word?

◉ Have you ever been taught how to use God's Word to fight temptation?

◉ What lie are you believing about yourself and your life right now? Create a table with two columns. On the left side, write down a lie you're believing. In the right-side column, write down the truth of God's Word that replaces that lie.

Today's Take Home Point

God's Word won't prove itself powerful in your life until God's Word becomes a part of your life.

Final Thought

◉ What is God inviting you to as it pertains to your time with Him daily?

Day 4: Even When I Fail

Reading: Galatians 3:15–26

Theme: Jesus is my provision for victory when I fail.

What about when failure rears its ugly head? What happens when Bible study is done and I'm left in a desert of temptation all by my lonesome self?

Despite how badly I want to conquer sin in my life and leave the desert of temptation, it often feels as if I'm stuck in a rental agreement I can't break. I long to move out, but I still find myself powerless against the evil one.

If you've been stuck in the desert of failure against temptation, today's lesson will encourage you. Just as we've been learning for the last few weeks, it's not our own valiant efforts against sin that will save us; it's God's faithfulness to us, despite our failure, that will.

📍 Let's spend some time in the Bible and write down what Christ has already accomplished for us. Read 1 Corinthians 15:53–57. Explain what our victory hinges upon.

Jesus' victory over Satan broke the power of sin for us. He fought the evil one on our behalf. He defeated sin and the law on our behalf. Because of His victory, we stand victorious today too.

Most of us act as if our victory depends on us. If we could just get it right, God will finally be pleased. If we could just make it a day without sinning, everything will be all right. But we can't get it right. We can't live perfectly. Only Jesus can. It's a matter of faith.

While most New Testament believers claim to live by faith, the reality is that few really understand what that looks like. Most of us are just like the people of Israel, always trying but never quite able to live up to God's law.

But there is a better way. His name is Jesus! In Christ, we are no longer governed by the law. The power of the law has been broken. Galatians 3 beautifully summarizes much of what we've been learning in the last few weeks together.

◉ Read Galatians 3:15–26. What happened to the law after Jesus came?

◉ Read Romans 4:13–17. What have God's promises to His people always depended upon?

◉ Read Galatians 2:20. What is the secret to the Christian life?

Incredible!

Faith. It all boils down to faith. We can go all the way back to Genesis 12 and see that God's way with His people has always been about faith. Abraham's faith rested on the belief that God would someday send a Savior through his seed, a Savior who would save the world. Though the people of God in the Old Testament were bound by the law, the promise of the coming Messiah was the hope that sustained those who truly knew God.

But what about when we fail? I'm glad you asked.

○ Read Hebrews 2:14–18. How does Jesus' victory over temptation help us when we're tempted?

○ Read Hebrews 4:14–16. What confidence does Christ's victory over temptation and sin give us?

I believe the church is full of Christians who are too afraid to approach God's throne of grace because they still struggle to believe God's faithfulness. We make it about us. We have the power of Christ in us, not because we have earned it or have proven ourselves able to stand victorious over sin, but because of what Jesus has done on our behalf.

Because Jesus conquered the evil one, the power of sin has been broken.

It was love that led Jesus to the desert, full of the Holy Spirit, to be tempted by Satan. It was that same love that led Jesus to the cross to be crucified for our sin.

○ When you consider the deep love of God for you, are you motivated to keep on sinning because you know forgiveness is yours already, or do you long for even more obedience?

God's love for us is incredible.

It's this love that called Abraham out of Haran into the unknown wilderness.

It's this love that compelled Moses to leave the wilderness behind and go back for his people. It's this love that heard the groaning of God's people in their bondage and delivered them from Egypt.

It's this love that led the people of Israel straight to the wilderness to help them get stronger. It's this love that remained true to His promises despite the hardness of His people. It's this love that continued to yearn for His people even after they rejected Him.

It's this love that caused Jesus to humble Himself and be willing to be born as a human. It's this love that fasted forty days in the wilderness in order to begin His conquest of the evil one on our behalf and eventually defeat the power of sin over us. It's this love that hung on a tree, wounded and pierced for our transgressions. It's this love that finds us in our desert places when we're covered with the shame of our own recurring failures.

God's faithfulness to us is motivated by His love for us.

Let's go back to Matthew 4:1–11. While of course Jesus is our greatest example to follow, He is so much more. So many Bible studies and sermons focus on the strategies Jesus used to overcome the evil one. I've made the mistake of thinking that if I just used the same strategies Jesus used, I'd be in good shape. Life has taught me that even with the best strategies, I can still fail.

What we need is not a handbook on how to overcome temptation. What we need is a Savior.

The point of Matthew 4 is to show us that we have a Savior who was faithful enough to overcome Satan. Jesus is our substitute in our fight against temptation. You are not in this desert alone. You have been crucified with Christ. It is Jesus who now lives in you and fights your battles.

Turning the tide on your failure against temptation is much less about what you do and all about what you believe. Your victory rests in understanding that God's faithfulness to you is best seen in the desert of temptation as you bow your knee to Jesus and allow His victory to sustain you.

You and I would never have been able to overcome sin, so Jesus had to do it for us. You and I will never be strong enough to face the evil one. Jesus had to face him for us.

This is a radical truth to absorb. If your strategy to fight sin has been to make a list of the three ways Jesus overcame Satan and try to do the same, no wonder you keep failing. You'll never be able to defeat the evil one. You need a Savior!

This is an incredible principle that will take you a lifetime to learn. As long as you continue to think of Jesus as a *means* to your victory, you'll stay stuck in defeat in the desert of temptation. It's only as you yield your whole self to Christ that you're able to stand in His victory, no matter how fierce the howling wind of temptation that comes your way.

The real battle we are facing is not a battle against sin. It's the battle of yielding our all to Jesus. Won't you surrender your all to Him today?

Let's Make This Personal

📍 What has been your strategy to overcome sin in your life? Has it worked?

📍 How have you handled your failure against sin so far?

📍 Is it easier for you to feel God's love for you when you offer Him your perfect behavior? How does today's teaching free you from this idea and invite you into freedom?

📍 What still stands in the way of your freedom? What areas of your life are you still refusing to surrender to Jesus?

Today's Take Home Point

Christ isn't merely an example to follow
but a Savior to bow down to.

Final Thought

📍 What is God's invitation to you in the places of your failure?

Day 5: Forever Faithful

Reading: Matthew 26:36–46

Theme: Eventually, the desert season will end, but God's faithfulness never will.

I've taken a lot of classes in my lifetime, and I can attest that no lesson is as good as the final lesson. It's a time to celebrate and review all that we've learned and accomplished.

This is our last day of homework together. I can't believe how quickly our time has come to an end. Before we summarize some of the key points we've been learning as we've tracked the footsteps of God through the desert, let's consider some final thoughts about Jesus in the wilderness of temptation.

Read Luke 4:13. What does this verse say about Satan's plans for Jesus' future?

On this side of heaven, the devil never stops attacking God's children. Just as he did with Jesus, he will keep looking for an opportune time to attack us again. It's why we must never let our guard down. Although God is the final authority on what happens to His children, the pressure of temptation won't stop until we see Jesus face to face someday.

As we continue to consider the life of Jesus, let's think about how else Satan tried to derail Christ and God's purpose for Him.

Read Matthew 16:21–23. Why did Jesus call Peter *Satan*?

📍 What can you learn about Satan's ultimate goal as you think about the words of Jesus in response to Peter?

📍 Read Matthew 26:36–46. The garden of Gethsemane is its own desert place. How was Satan attacking Jesus in the garden of Gethsemane?

📍 How did Jesus resist Satan in the garden of Gethsemane?

Jesus did indeed win the battle in the garden of Gethsemane. He did it by surrendering His will to the will of His Father. He did it because He trusted His Father even in the face of an inconceivable immediate future. Although the road ahead would lead to His death on the cross, His surrender in the garden was what paved the way for us to call God our Father too. Because Jesus died, we'll never have to!

God's faithfulness to His people is magnified at the cross. His faithfulness to His people is what led Jesus to die on Calvary for our sake. Christ's faithfulness is what made a way for us to enter the Father's presence. Because Christ was faithful, we have access to the Father and can approach His throne of grace with confidence.

Q Read Hebrews 10:19–23. What can you learn about God's faithfulness in these verses?

One of the key lessons we've learned together is that it's not by accident that we find our-selves in desert places. God intentionally leads us to the desert places and allows us to remain there for a season. His goal is our ultimate transformation. God's greatest tool to change us is the desert, because the desert is the ideal place for us to see God's faithfulness. God uses our painful places as the pathways to our healing. He uses our painful places to teach us to depend on Him even more. He transforms our painful places into palaces of communion with Him.

Q What two or three verses or scriptural principles about God's faithfulness stick out in your mind as you think about all we've studied together in the last five weeks?

We've spent time in a number of desert places so far: the desert of testing and claiming God's promises, the desert of brokenness and defeat, the desert of mercy, the desert of waiting, the desert of temptation, the desert of failure.

Q In which desert place has God met you the most?

Christian transformation is not a onetime event. It's a process. While we might be motivated to change at the end of a Bible study, the process of transformation takes time. Peter, despite being called Satan by Jesus, understood this. Because he himself was so radically transformed by Jesus, the words in his letter are so much more powerful.

◉ Read 1 Peter 1:3–8. What does Peter tell us is the purpose of our trials?

◉ What does Peter remind us we're still waiting for as children of God?

◉ What should motivate our joy as Christians?

◉ How would you describe your love for Christ today compared to the first day of this study?

◉ What are some things about God that have stirred your heart to love Him more deeply?

My life verse is Philippians 1:6. I was a teenager when I underlined this verse and committed my life to Jesus. I was so sure of everything in those days. That was life before the desert places. Today, I've marched through too many desert seasons to keep track of. Some seasons have been longer than others. Some seasons have been expected, and others have taken me by surprise. I've kicked and screamed my way out of some of my desert places. But I'm still here, more convinced than ever of God's faithfulness.

📍 Read Philippians 1:6. According to this verse, whose job is it to transform you and keep you until you see Jesus?

📍 According to this verse, how long will God remain faithful to His children?

The pressure is not on you! You can take a deep breath. God promises to do the heavy lifting of keeping you through the desert and changing you into His likeness.

God uses our painful places as the pathways to our healing.

The same God who faithfully led Abraham out of Haran is leading you today. His covenant with you through Jesus stands forever. The same God who led the people of Israel for forty years through the wilderness is leading you too. The same God who poured His love and mercy on His undeserving people continues to pour His love on you through Christ. The same God who wept for John the Baptist after using him so mightily is the God who cares for you today. The same God who rose victorious over death and sin stands victorious on your behalf today.

You don't have to try so hard anymore. You don't have to impress God with your performance. You don't have to worry about your future. You don't have to wonder what you did wrong or where God is in your pain.

If there's anything I've learned about God through the desert, it's that nothing and no one can ever stand against the power of God's love for His children.

He is forever faithful!

Let's Make This Personal

What are the two or three biggest lessons you've learned about God's faithfulness in this Bible study?

What are some of the specific ways God has been faithful to you in your desert places?

Where in your life do you still long to change?

Today's Take Home Point

You can rest assured that God's
faithfulness to you will never stop.

Final Thought

📍 What is God's invitation to you as you conclude this Bible study series?

Praying through Scripture—Week 5

Taste of Victory

Matthew 4:1–11

Then Jesus was led up by the Spirit into the wilderness to be tempted by the devil. And after fasting forty days and forty nights, he was hungry. And the tempter came and said to him, "If you are the Son of God, command these stones to become loaves of bread." But he answered, "It is written,

"'Man shall not live by bread alone,
but by every word that comes from the mouth of God.'"

Then the devil took him to the holy city and set him on the pinnacle of the temple and said to him, "If you are the Son of God, throw yourself down, for it is written,

"'He will command his angels concerning you,'

and

"'On their hands they will bear you up,
lest you strike your foot against a stone.'"

Jesus said to him, "Again it is written, 'You shall not put the Lord your God to the test.'" Again, the devil took him to a very high mountain and showed him all the kingdoms of the world and their glory. And he said to him, "All these I will give you, if you will fall down and worship me." Then Jesus said to him, "Be gone, Satan! For it is written,

"'You shall worship the Lord your God
and him only shall you serve.'"

Then the devil left him, and behold, angels came and were ministering to him.

Read the passage out loud once.

Now close your eyes and take a few deep breaths. Pray with me: "O God, I pray that You will help me to hear You speak during this time of meditation on Your Word. I open my hands to You. I open my ears to You."

Pause for eight to ten seconds.

Describe the scene of this encounter. Take a deep breath. What does it smell like in the desert? What does it feel like? How hot is it? You've been fasting for forty days. You haven't had any food for over a month. Describe how you feel physically. Have you ever felt this weak or this thirsty? What are you praying in these moments? What do you expect will happen?

Read the passage again.

Pause for eight to ten seconds.

When the tempter suddenly appears, how do you react? Do you feel afraid? Now imagine the same events, but instead of facing the tempter alone, you look up and you see Jesus standing in front of you. He's defending you. He's standing up for you. How does the presence of Jesus change how you feel as you face the tempter?

You listen in on the conversation between the tempter and Jesus. Are you surprised by the fact that the evil one is using the Scriptures to make his case? Are you wishing that Jesus would in fact turn the stones into bread? How hungry do you feel in that moment? Why do you think Jesus refuses to do so? Are you disappointed that Jesus refuses to give in to the evil one?

Pause for five to eight seconds.

You keep watching. The tempter then challenges Jesus to jump from the top of the temple. Why do you think he's asking Jesus to do that? What does that have to do with you? In what ways do you long to be spectacular? You remember the things you've been praying about. You've begged God for a spectacular breakthrough. Could your desire for the spectacular be less about God and more about you? How does Jesus' response to the tempter surprise you? Are you disappointed in His response, or can you find peace?

Pause for five to eight seconds.

You keep listening. The tempter still comes after Jesus. You're tired even thinking about it. You're still dying of thirst. You just want this to end. You look at Jesus. Does He seem tired? Does He seem afraid?

This third encounter is even more baffling. The tempter is promising Jesus everything. Something tells you by now this is impossible. You're happy to hear Jesus' answer, but you start to wonder. Where in your life have you been bending the knee to Satan's promises in the hopes of getting what you want *now*? Think about the ways you've refused to worship God when it's been inconvenient. Think about the ways you've compromised your beliefs because things got too hard. You're reminded that Satan cannot give you what is not his to begin with.

Pretty soon, Satan leaves you.

What fills your heart as you consider what Jesus has just accomplished for you in the desert? You look around and notice angels surrounding you. You're so caught up in the moment, you forget that you're hungry. You forget that you're thirsty. What do you feel in that moment? What goes through your mind and heart? How does the experience with Jesus in the wilderness change you? Do you feel stronger? Do you feel more dependent?

📍 As you wrap up this exercise, write down what you would tell Jesus after this encounter in the wilderness. If you could express your heart to Jesus, what would you say?

Session 6

Overcoming in Desert Places

Matthew 4:1-11

Watch the session 6 video now. The video is available at DavidCCook.org/access, with access code DesertPlaces.

1. In order to live victoriously, I must understand the _____ raging in desert places.

2. In order to live victoriously, I must follow the _____ of Jesus in desert places.

3. In order to live victoriously, I must embrace Christ's _____ rather than my own failure.

4. In order to live victoriously, I must continue to expect God's _____ to help me make it through desert places.

Video Discussion Guide

After watching the video, discuss the following questions in your group.

- How does knowing that God leads His beloved to the wilderness of temptation encourage you or frustrate you?

- In what areas of your life does temptation come most frequently?

- "Sin always promises what it can't provide." How does this statement ring true for you? What's an example where you have seen this play out?

- When have you ever experienced the power of God's Word in overcoming temptation, and what was that like?

- God's faithfulness doesn't depend on your performance but on His character. How does this principle give you hope today?

Final Thought

Well, we made it! It's been so great to spend the last six weeks with you. I hope you have found yourself drawn closer to the Lord. I trust that your faith roots are deeper than they were when we started. And although we've never met, I feel like we're already friends.

As your new friend, I would love to stay in touch with you. There are a number of ways for us to stay connected:

1. Social media: Follow me on Instagram (instagram.com/livingwithpowerministries) and Facebook (facebook.com/livingwithpower).
2. Check out more Bible study resources at www.livingwithpower.org.
3. Send me an email and tell me how God has used this study in your life: lina@livingwithpower.org.

If you're feeling a little tearful at our parting, don't worry—we will meet again soon with my follow-up study of God's faithfulness, coming soon from David C Cook.

Big hug. Little kisses.

Lina

Leader's Guide

Thank you for deciding to shepherd a *Through the Desert* group. I am grateful for your willingness to share yourself and to help other women dig deeper into God's Word. I hope this guide will help you as you study God's Word together.

There is a general flow to each group session that brings comfort in its predictability.

1. Invite discussion of each woman's personal study time from the past week. This leader's guide will suggest specific questions from the week to reflect on and answer with your group. You don't have to feel pressure to use all the questions each week. Instead use them as a springboard for discussion about what God has done in your group members' hearts that week.
2. Watch the video and take notes on what you hear.
3. Discuss the questions provided on the group discussion page.
4. Invite prayer requests, pray, and dismiss.

Ideally, you will want to schedule at least an hour each week for the study to have time for both watching the video teaching and group discussion afterward.

Tips on Leading

1. Pray. Nothing will move the hearts of the women in your group like prayer. Set aside time each week to pray for each woman in your group. Get to know your women and bring their needs before the Lord regularly.

2. Guide. Your job isn't to change the women in your group but to help guide them. Listen carefully to what each woman shares. Be willing to be vulnerable, and you'll set the tone for your group to do the same. Lead by example. Be consistent and trustworthy.

3. Connect. Be creative to connect with the women in your group during the week. Use social media as well as texts and email to encourage your women, share prayer requests, and stay connected with them.

Session 1

Use this first session to build relationships with your group. Get familiar with the content of the study, including the video. Preview the study with the women in your group so they know what's coming.

1. Be sure each woman in your group has a copy of *Through the Desert*.

2. Remind your group participants of the importance of keeping anything discussed in the small group within the small group. You want to be sure everyone feels comfortable sharing.

3. Invite each member of your group to introduce herself and share something so everyone can begin to build relationships.

4. Ask what drew each member to the study.

5. Ask the women to share what they already know about the desert places and how God reveals His faithfulness to His people through the desert.

6. Ask each woman to share what she hopes to learn in this study.

7. Before you begin the video, ask each woman to silently think about the desert places in their lives right now. Have they ever doubted God's faithfulness to them in their desert places?

8. Watch the introduction video and answer the discussion questions in the group guide.

9. Instruct the women to complete the session 1 homework section in the study guide and to come ready to discuss it next week.

10. Pray and dismiss.

Session 2

1. Questions to ask your group:

a. What stuck out the most for you in this week's study? It may be a verse, sentence, thought, or idea.

b. Read Genesis 12:1–9 together. What was it about the call of God to Abraham that motivated such radical faith?

c. How does Abraham's story of faith encourage you to follow God more completely?

d. Describe a time in your life when you stepped out by faith in obedience to God not knowing where you were going.

e. While Abraham's faith came under the Old Covenant, you and I have been given a New Covenant in Jesus Christ. How is the promise of the New Covenant impacting your life?

f. How does understanding that Jesus is our hope remove any sense of disappointment in unfulfilled dreams?

g. Share some of the sacred places where you have encountered God intimately.

h. Abraham's response to famine was fear. Where in your life do you feel a "famine," and what has been your response to the famine?

2. Watch the session 2 video and discuss the questions in the group guide.

3. Pray and dismiss.

Session 3

1. Questions to ask your group:

a. What stuck out the most for you in this week's study? It may be a verse, sentence, thought, or idea.

b. Read Exodus 13:17–22 together. Why did God lead the people of Israel to the desert instead of taking them the shorter way to the Promised Land?

c. As you consider your own desert places, how has it encouraged you to understand that God has a purpose for the desert?

d. God gives us compass headings as we make our way through the desert. While the people of Israel were given a pillar of cloud by day and a pillar of fire by night, what are some of the landmarks or guidance you've been given?

e. What stands in the way of your seeing God's presence in your life right now?

f. How was the Red Sea experience an opportunity for God to get glory over Pharaoh through the people of Israel?

g. Where in your life are you waiting for a parting of the Red Sea? How did this week's lesson encourage you to keep on waiting for a breakthrough?

h. Exodus 15:1–21 was a desert song in response to God's miraculous intervention at the Red Sea. What song has filled your heart this week in meditating on God's faithfulness?

2. Watch the session 3 video and discuss the questions in the group guide.

3. Pray and dismiss.

Session 4

1. Questions to ask your group:

a. What stuck out the most for you in this week's study? It may be a verse, sentence, thought, or idea.

b. Read Jeremiah 31:1–5. What was your favorite verse in this week's passage of Scripture?

c. As you consider the people of Israel, in what ways do they remind you of yourself?

d. What effect did the words of the Lord in Jeremiah 31 have on you?

e. Have you ever found yourself in a place where you doubted God's willingness to give you a second chance? How did you get past that place?

f. Where in your life are you lacking joy?

g. Is there anything you're still waiting for to experience joy in the Lord?

2. Watch the session 4 video and discuss the questions in the group guide.

3. Pray and dismiss.

Session 5

1. Questions to ask your group:

a. What stuck out the most for you in this week's study? It may be a verse, sentence, thought, or idea.

b. Read Matthew 3:1–6. What are some things you learned about John the Baptist? How did his life impact you this week?

c. What was John the Baptist's main message? Did it surprise you that the people responded positively to his message?

d. Have you ever gotten to the place in your life where you were desperate enough to listen to God's voice? Are you there right now?

e. What distractions keep you from waking up to God?

f. What does being spiritually awake look like for you?

g. How have your desert places been an invitation for you to change?

2. Watch the session 5 video and discuss the questions in the group guide.

3. Pray and dismiss.

Session 6

This is the last week with your group. Congratulate the women for finishing strong. Share highs and lows. Take time to celebrate the wins. Challenge the women in your group to continue to study God's Word and to share what they've learned with the people in their lives.

1. Questions to ask your group:

a. What stuck out the most for you in this week's study? It may be a verse, sentence, thought, or idea.

b. Read Matthew 4:1–11. Why do you think God allowed Jesus to go to the wilderness of temptation?

c. What are some of the things you learned about Jesus this week?

d. What emotions fill your heart when you consider that God allowed His beloved Son in whom He was well pleased to enter a season of temptation?

e. How does the encounter between Jesus and Satan encourage you to stand strong in your desert of temptation?

f. What lies are you believing in your life, and what are the truths you can use to overcome those lies?

g. What have you learned about God's faithfulness to you in this week's lesson?

2. Watch the session 6 video and discuss the questions in the group guide. (There are no homework questions for this final week.)

3. Pray and dismiss.

Answers to blanks in the lesson main points provided in the session videos.

Session 1: Introduction

Genesis 1–2

> 1. faithfulness
> 2. difficult places
> 3. purpose

Session 2: Invited into the Desert

Genesis 12:1–9

> 1. covenant
> 2. receiving
> 3. the desert

Session 3: Purpose in the Desert

Exodus 13:17–22

> 1. for your good
> 2. pointing the way
> 3. believe
> 4. depth

Session 4: Mercy in the Desert

Jeremiah 31:2–14

> 1. God's love
> 2. efforts
> 3. my promises
> 4. commitment

Session 5: The Gift of Desert Places

Luke 3:1–22

1. need

2. brokenness

3. important

4. equipped

Session 6: Overcoming in Desert Places

Matthew 4:1–11

1. battle

2. example

3. perfection

4. faithfulness

Through the Desert

A STUDY ON GOD'S FAITHFULNESS

SIX-SESSION VIDEO SERIES

LINA
ABUJAMRA

VIDEO SERIES ACCESS

Link: https://davidccook.org/prd/desert-places

Access code: DesertPlaces

Notes

1. Merriam-Webster Dictionary, s.v. "faithful," www.merriam-webster.com/dictionary/faithful.

2. Mark Jones, "What Is Covenant?," Ligonier, April 25, 2014, www.ligonier.org/learn/articles/what-covenant.

3. The chart is compiled from the following scholarly works: C. C. Newman, "Covenant, New Covenant: Paul, Acts, Hebrews," *The IVP Dictionary of the New Testament*, ed. Daniel G. Reid (Downers Grove, IL: InterVarsity, 2004), 247–48; Barry C. Joslin, *Hebrews, Christ, and the Law* (Colorado Springs: Paternoster, 2008), 253–55; David L. Allen, *Hebrews*, in The New American Commentary, Vol. 35 (Nashville: B&H Publishing Group, 2010), 451–52.

4. Oswald Chambers, *My Utmost for His Highest*, January 6 entry, https://utmost.org/classic/worship-classic/2/.

5. Holmes Rolston, "Biblical wilderness—Midbar, arabah and eremos," https://mountainscholar.org/bitstream /handle/10217/172809/FACFPHIL_Rolston_BiblicalWilderness.pdf?sequence=1&isAllowed=y.

6. Vern Poythress, "Theophany," The Gospel Coalition, accessed May 25, 2022, www.thegospelcoalition.org /essay/theophany/.

7. E. A. Andrews, *Harper's Latin Dictionary* (New York: American Book Company, 1907), 817.

8. Joni Eareckson Tada and Steve Estes, *When God Weeps* (Grand Rapids, MI: Zondervan, 1997), 84.

9. Inspired by "You Are My King (Amazing Love)" by Billy James Foote, on Phillips, Craig, and Dean, *Let My Words Be Few*, Hal Leonard Corporation, 2001.

10. David Guzik, "Luke 3—The Work of John the Baptist," Enduring Word, accessed May 25, 2022, https://enduringword.com/bible-commentary/luke-3/.

11. "What Is the Pre-Christian History of the Baptismal Ceremony?," *Christianity Today*, August 8, 2008, www.christianitytoday.com/history/2008/august/what-is-pre-christian-history-of-baptismal-ceremony.html.

12. John Piper, "I Baptize You with Water," Desiring God, May 4, 1997, www.desiringgod.org/messages /i-baptize-you-with-water.

13. Witness Lee, *Life-Study of Luke*, The Bible—Recovery Version, https://bibleread.online/all-books-by -Watchman-Nee-and-Witness-Lee/book-life-study-of-luke-Witness-Lee-read-online/10/.

14. David Roach, "Bible Reading Drops during Social Distancing," *Christianity Today*, July 22, 2020, www.christianitytoday.com/news/2020/july/state-of-bible-reading-coronavirus-barna-abs.html.

15. Aaron Earls, "More Americans Are Reading the Bible. Now What?," Lifeway Research, May 28, 2021, https://lifewayresearch.com/2021/05/28/more-americans-are-reading-the-bible-now-what/.

DO YOU LONG TO SEE REVIVAL IN YOUR CHURCH?

ARE YOU DESPERATE FOR A FRESH MOVE OF GOD IN YOUR LIFE?

ARE YOU LOOKING FOR HOPE IN A BROKEN WORLD?

INVITE LINA TO SPEAK AT YOUR EVENT

Lina's mission is to ignite hope in the people of God through the clear and unapologetic teaching of God's Word.

Lina fell in love with teaching the Bible when she was the women's ministry director at a megachurch. Now a popular Bible teacher and podcaster, she speaks extensively at conferences, retreats, and colleges around the world. Her desire is to inspire passion for Jesus in the hearts of God's people and help them experience the beauty of His healing power so they can live in the fullness of who He is calling them to be.

Familiar with pain and brokenness, Lina has authenticity, relatable storytelling, and solid biblical teaching that connects with audiences of all ages and backgrounds.

INVITE LINA:
livingwithpower.org/speaking

LIVING WITH POWER

WE EQUIP CHRISTIANS
TO LIVE WITH POWER BY...

Unapologetically teaching God's Word, providing discipleship resources,
and giving medical and humanitarian aid in disaster areas.

LIVINGWITHPOWER.ORG

estherpress

Our journey invites us deeper into God's Word, where wisdom waits to renew our minds and where the Holy Spirit meets us in discernment that empowers bold action for such a time as this.

If we have the courage to say yes to our calling and no to everything else, will the world be ready?

JOIN US IN COURAGEOUS LIVING

Your Esther Press purchase helps to equip, encourage, and disciple women around the globe with practical assistance and spiritual mentoring to help them become strong leaders and faithful followers of Jesus.

An imprint of

DAVID C COOK

transforming lives together